My search became an obsession. If I saw someone on the street who looked like me, I'd turn and follow her. If someone idly said to me, "you look like someone I know," I felt I had to pursue it further. I'd tell her I was adopted and that I didn't know who I looked like, I didn't know who my parents were.

Maybe I have a sister; maybe I have a mother or father somewhere. "Is it possible you've seen one of them?" I'd ask that person's age and what precisely they looked like and where they lived. The more questions I asked, the less cooperative the person became.

What a curious, naive, and compulsive pattern this was—and yet I have received hundreds of letters from adoptees who do the same thing....

The Search
for
Anna Fisher

by Florence Fisher

FAWCETT CREST • NEW YORK

To my adoptive uncle,
ABRAHAM SCHECHTER,
with happy memories
of a lifetime
of love

Acknowledgments

There are trying days in the lives of all of us, times we might be unable to weather without the support of those we love, or a kind word from a stranger. To Timothy F. Beard and Frank E. Bradley of the New York Public Library, Local History and Genealogy Department, who will never again be strangers, my appreciation and affection for the kindness and patience with which they always answered my questions.

I am indebted to Nick Lyons for his expert criticism and assistance.

I am deeply grateful to Arthur Fields for his decision to publish this book, for the wisdom with which he guided me during its most difficult stages, and for his sincere concern for me as a person as well as a writer.

To my husband, Stan, for his encouragement and constant support during the final, trying days of my search, and for never questioning my right to know . . . thank you.

F.F.

Oh, why does the wind blow upon me so wild?
Is it because I'm nobody's child?

—PHILA HENRIETTA CASE

Prologue

―――――――――――――――――――――――――

I'm sure you can understand my wanting to see some-
one in this world who is actually flesh and blood
related to me.

―An adoptee

Four years ago I was in an automobile accident. Suddenly the brakes failed. I pressed the pedal frantically and
saw the other car dead ahead, with its driver pressed
against the wheel and some children jumping up and
down in the front seat. I swerved and a telephone pole
raced toward me. My last thought in the second before
the crash was: "Oh, God, I'm going to die and I don't
know who I am."

I was forty then, a wife and the mother of one grown
son, but I had spent almost twenty years trying to answer
that question.

As I lay in the sterile white outpatient room, with three
broken ribs, glad to be alive but still terrified at the
thought of what might have happened, a nurse came over
to my bed with a clipboard full of routine questions.

"Are there any hereditary diseases in your family?" she asked.

How could I answer her? I was an adoptee.

Perhaps it was the accident, the brush with death and the thought that I might die still not knowing. But that could only have provided the final impetus to conclude a search for my natural parents that had begun twenty years earlier, on the night I learned I was adopted.

Though my childhood had not been pleasant, that was not what motivated my search. Other adoptees I have come to know, who sincerely loved their adoptive families, have no less a desire to know their origins. What is more natural than the desire to learn something of one's heritage? All children love to be regaled with anecdotes and details about their parents and grandparents. They look at their parents and try to find something of themselves in the way these people walk and talk, in their interests and talents, in their strengths and flaws. Such information provides a frame for their lives, and a continuity with their pasts. It confirms and solidifies their images of themselves. "There is ample evidence that the adopted child retains the need for seeking his ancestry for a long time," said the Council on Child Health of the American Academy of Pediatrics in a recent issue of *Pediatrics* magazine. "What he is really seeking is to achieve a unity and persistence of personality in spite of the break in the continuity of his life."

A little more than a year ago, in an attempt to establish contact with other adoptees, to share with them what I had learned and perhaps by so doing to save them some of the heartbreak and waste that I had experienced, I placed this simple newspaper ad:

> Adult who was an adopted child desires contact with other adoptees to exchange views on adoptive situation and for mutual assistance in search for natural parents.

The response was overwhelming. Letters poured in from all over the country, letters expressing the same hunger to know that at one time I had thought was mine alone. Later, having seen me on television or read one of several articles about me that appeared in major magazines and newspapers, still more people wrote to me.

"While I was reading about you, I felt I was reading about myself," one woman wrote.

"My life has been good," wrote another, "but I cannot fill the void caused by not knowing who I look like, walk like, or whose mannerisms I have."

Some expressed fear that their adoptive parents would learn of their desire to search for their natural parents; others feared the reactions their real fathers or mothers might have, and had a passionate desire not to hurt them. But all wanted to know—some fiercely, some with quiet determination. "I am sixty-four years old, please help me before I die." "Thirty-six years of searching and I have uncovered nothing." "There is no help anywhere." "Sometimes when I walk down a street and see someone who looks like me . . . I pause and think, *Could that be my own mother?*"

More than other people, adoptees fear the consequences of venting their true feelings. They were cast out once, and many still feel the mark of the outcast on them. Fearing the possibility of being found unworthy or ungrateful, they lie low. A number of people asked me to reply in unmarked envelopes so their families would not know of their deep but hidden desires to seek out other adoptees and to search for their natural parents. In this, I was different: I never resented the fact of my adoption, and I never doubted my right to know my origins.

But there were other letters from adoptive parents— disturbing, hostile letters that flamed with hate.

"You are shallow and ungrateful," one woman wrote me. "Your adoptive parents didn't think of your heritage or the traits you have that could have destroyed them."

"Be thankful." "You are a crazy, meddling witch." "Act your age—get off this kick." "How utterly ridiculous." "You may find your father and I bet he will want no part of you." "Why do you want to find out you were born in a sewer if you grew up in a garden?"

Be thankful. Be grateful. Don't meddle. Act your age. You've come from the gutter. You'll find only further rejection. "You were rotten and dirty from the day you were born," I was told. "Once a bastard, always a bastard." They were familiar sentiments. I had heard them all before—in person.

I am not steel.

But comments such as these are not the only forms of resistance I and other adoptees encounter. Some, of course, are legal: adoption records are sealed by the state, and can only be opened for "good cause"; original birth certificates are also sealed, and altered copies, listing the adoptive parents as the only parents, are issued by state authority; adoption agencies maintain a policy of upholding the secrecy of all parties. They pride themselves on the confidentiality of their services. Certainly adoptive parents have a right to peace of mind; legal protections should remain in force during an adoptee's childhood. But need the security of the adoptive home be threatened in *any* way if the child, when he reaches *adulthood*, wants to know his heritage? Most of the resistance encountered had as its source a challenge to my *right* to know. A great mythological king once said: "My mind abideth strong/To know the roots that grew to Oedipus." My search, and the search of every other adoptee who is not satisfied with half knowledge about himself, is for the same hidden roots.

Not long ago I flew to California to meet a man I had never met. The man was eighteen years older than I, and during the two weeks we spent together he was frequently taken for my escort. We went to a Polynesian restaurant together that first night and sat looking at each other for hours, peering at every detail of each other's face. He told me of the stunt work he did, the movies he's worked on, the actors and actresses he knew. "Bring my daughter the menu," he said to the waiter. "Let's see what my daughter wants." And later: "Bring my daughter a glass of water"; "my daughter might want more bread." He seemed positively unable to say the word often enough, and I laughed and chided him lightly, and said the waiter must think it's some kind of a joke, and he laughed and said, when the waiter returned, "I'm sure my daughter wants some dessert."

As I listened to him, I couldn't believe I'd found this absolutely delightful man. I felt so proud of him. It was such a pleasure to be with this warm, laughing, bubbly person. It was all a fantasy, but it was real, too—blessedly real. And I felt I'd earned him.

"You're far away," he said once, sensitive to my slightest mood. "Where were you?"

I said: "I was thinking of the past." All that evening I had had the sensation of the past, the present, and the future slamming together inside me.

"I know about your past," he said. "What can I tell you?" He told me everything I wanted to know—openly, fully, without more than a touch of regret.

We talked that night until three in the morning. He's a talker and I'm a talker, and we walked up and down Hollywood Boulevard, holding hands and chattering incessantly, often both at the same time. We wanted to cram a lifetime of talk into those short two weeks.

The next day he took me to his studio and introduced me to everyone. "This is my daughter," he told a friend. "Isn't she beautiful?"

"I didn't know you had a daughter, Fred."

"Of course I have a daughter! I've always had a daughter."

He took me to the gate man who had let him in and

out of the studio for forty years, to his barber, to the luncheonette. Several times he drew forth a picture of me when I was three years old, which I'd given to him, and displayed it proudly. He listened ruefully while I gaily whispered: "Let's get out of here before they lock you up. You're totally nuts!"

We went to Malibu Beach one morning to visit Will Rogers' house, and he took photographs of me in every conceivable pose. Look up. Look down. Turn your face this way, Florence. That way. Look sideways. He did everything but take one with a lollipop hanging out of my mouth.

He was like a father with his little girl, and I loved being that little girl. We went to the Farmers' Market, and walked through the stalls of vegetables, fruits, and exotic foods, and when he had to get back to go on a job interview, he said: "Have to take you back now."

"What for?" I asked. "I'll stay here. You can pick me up later."

"What do you mean you'll stay here? *Alone?*"

I tried to keep from laughing. "Of course alone!"

He wasn't at all sure it would work. "You'll be careful when you cross Hollywood Boulevard? You won't talk to strangers, will you? There are all sorts of people walking around here, you know."

I shook my head and began to laugh convulsively. "Look at me," I said. "I'm not two years old."

"I know, I know," he said with mock gruffness. "But be careful, anyhow. Promise?"

"Yes," I said, taking his hand, "I promise."

Toward the end of the second week, we went to Disneyland together. What a wonderful, impossible day that was! We went to Fantasy Land and took the Caribbean Cruise, sitting in the first row, getting pelted with waves until we were two hysterically laughing drowned rats, watching pirates bury gold and burn towns and laugh and dance with such animation you'd have thought they were real. *Is all this really happening to me?* I thought. *Is it me—and is it really him?* We took a motor boat out and knocked the other boats with abandon. We took the Jungle Cruise and stuffed ourselves with ice cream, popcorn, cotton candy, and frozen bananas. Only when he saw a father with a little girl would he grow quiet for a moment and squeeze my hand as if I were a little child, and then we'd skip off, smiling, laughing, talking without pause— and usually at the same time—as we had since I'd crossed the country to find this stranger who was not and had never been a stranger.

We were quiet and depressed the day I had to leave, though sporadically he'd look intently into my eyes and say: "My kid!" From the window of the airplane that would take me back to my home in New York, where I had a husband to love and an organization to run, I looked out and saw him standing quietly with his hands in his pockets, searching up for my window. He blew me a kiss and waved his right hand. I waved and whispered, not "good-bye" but *ciao.*

This was my natural father, and finding him more than justified the unspeakable search that had occupied almost my whole life. It was a search that had begun with a piece of paper I found when I was seven years old. That paper became a thorn in my brain, and I knew I would never have peace or joy until I got it out. Was I Florence Ladden, the name I'd always known, or was I the "Anna Fisher" listed on that piece of paper?

And who *was* Anna Fisher?

Who Is Anna Fisher?

One

****

I'll wonder for the rest of my life who I am.
　　　　　　　—An adopted woman, age fifty

My name was Florence Ladden. I was always a very small
girl, so small my parents could keep me in a crib until
I was ten years old, but I loved to sing and dance, and I
made up for my size with the volume of noise I made
and the mischief I got into. I always had a strong will and
a sense of what was rightfully mine. From my earliest
years I felt there was a mystery surrounding my life—
and, like any secret you know exists but cannot fathom,
that mystery haunted me.

The crib could not contain my spirit, and I knew that
some day I'd break the bars of the cage that secret doomed
me to. My only questions were, "How?" and "When?"

I lived with my father and mother, Rose and Harry
Ladden, in three rooms on the second floor of an apartment building in Brooklyn. There was a small square
foyer as you came in, and a large closet to the right. On
the shelf in this closet I kept all my Big Little books

because there was no room for them near my crib. Though I can't remember who taught me, I was reading fluently before I was five, and those Big Little books were my prized possessions. Uncle Abe often brought them for me in bulging pockets.

We had a kitchen, in which we ate; a living room in which my grandmother and Uncle Abe slept; and the bedroom, with its large double bed, walnut dresser, kidney-shaped vanity table with three adjustable mirror panels, and the crib in which I slept, bars up, until I was ten. My grandmother still had both feet in the Old World, and was a fixed and quite unpleasant presence in my life; but Uncle Abe, who took me for walks and let me help tend his pigeons, who smiled and saved silver Camels' wrappers for me and never forgot a birthday of mine, was the joy of my life.

I had three friends in the building, Beverly, BeeBee, and Elena. They always played with each other and sometimes, when my mother permitted me to, I played with them. It was always more pleasant to go to one of their apartments, or to the house next door. That's where the huge Italian family lived, a raft of them—all tawny-skinned and black-haired, and always singing. Their home was always full of song and good food and happy faces—and I loved to visit it.

The first hint I had that some dark secret surrounded my birth came when I was five; the day my mother enrolled me in kindergarten.

I can remember how she fixed my hair that morning. I had long curls, and she had combed out my hair, parted it on one side, and fastened a bright taffeta bow on the other. I remember that I had on a pink dress that day, and that we had an argument about whether I was to wear Mary Janes or Oxfords. Mother wanted me to wear the Oxfords, and I insisted I would wear the Mary Janes or go barefoot.

I won.

We walked the few blocks from our apartment house and entered the red-brick school building from the side. I can remember the hollow sound my little heels made on the wood slat floor. There were a few other women with their children, all sitting at their desks, in the room to which we were led. Some new ones came, some left the quiet room, and soon it was our turn. Mother sat down at the side of the registrar's desk; I stood beside her. I was terribly excited about going to school, where I knew I'd meet some friends and read a lot and draw, and I wanted to see and hear everything. I glanced at the many papers sprawled on the small brown desk.

"May we have Florence's birth certificate, Mrs. Ladden?" the registrar said. She was a dour, drab woman—very busy, very businesslike.

My mother put her hand on her purse—and then she drew her hand back as if she had touched a hot skillet.

What was wrong?

My mother turned to me and said: "Wait outside the door, Florence."

I looked at her closely. Something was very wrong. Why should she want me to leave the room? None of the other little girls, the ones who had gone before me, had been asked to leave the room. Why should I have to leave if *I* was going to school. I knew what "birth" meant, but the other word was long and hard to pronounce. The other word meant something important. And it was *mine*. Whatever it was, the woman had said it was "Florence's," and it had something to do with when I was born. I looked at my mother's face; I looked in her eyes. She was trying to hide something from me. She was *afraid*.

"I want to see it," I said, not moving from my place beside the desk.

I could see that my mother was growing angry. "Just wait outside the door, Florence," she said.

"Why can't I see it?" I asked. I searched my mother's pale yellow-green eyes. She looked slightly away from me.

I looked at her purse; she was holding it tightly in both hands, almost trying to hide it. I put my hands on my hips and clicked my Mary Janes on the floor, and then the registrar said something about my lack of discipline and I insisted that my mother wasn't going to go to the school, I was, and that I wanted to see my birth whatayoucallit. My mother took me by the arms and led me out the door. She did not have her purse; she had left it on the desk. She placed me forcibly on a wooden bench in the hallway, told me to stay there, and went back into the room quickly.

I sat there silently for a moment, looking at the closed door. What was that look in her eyes? I'd never seen her eyes like that before. What were they going to say about me in that room? Why couldn't I hear? Was there something wrong with me? I felt uneasy and began to squirm on the bench. After a few minutes, I got up slowly, looked both ways, and ran down the hall and out of the building. I wanted to get as far away as I could from her and from the school. For weeks I had looked forward to starting school, and now why was there this mystery, and why had I been sent from the room? There was a woman with a baby carriage in the street, and after running for a few minutes, I took up a position directly in front of the carriage, so no one would see me, and walked there for several hundred yards.

Half a block from our apartment house, there was a row of private wood-frame houses. I'd played in one of them with a little boy named Marshall, and before Marshall had moved in, we'd once gone to an Italian wedding in that house. Everyone sang and danced at the wedding, just like the big Italian family that lived in the house next to ours always sang and danced and laughed. The house had a wooden porch, and I wriggled under it, scurrying back into the darkness and then cowering behind a pillar. I didn't want to be found, not ever. I kept thinking of that strange look in my mother's eyes. She had been afraid that I'd see or hear and know something about my birth. But what, I wondered, could be wrong with how I was born?

There was dirt everywhere, and soon my pink dress was smudged in a dozen places. I heard my taffeta bow crinkle when it rubbed against a pillar or low board above me. It fell off and I hunted for it in the dirt. I looked down at my Mary Janes; they were filthy with dust and dirt.

I must have been there for hours; for when I saw the policeman's blue hat and then heard him say, "C'mon little girl," it was already late afternoon and the shadows had grown darker and I had grown hungry. I didn't like the dark; it made me feel I was buried alive. I didn't want to go back, and held tightly onto the pillar, but when the policeman put out his hand I looked back at the shadows and let go and went with him.

When I was delivered home, I found my mother in hysterics. My father was home, even though it was too early for him to have returned from work, and without a word he hauled me into the bedroom and took off his belt. He never beat me when Uncle Abe was home, but now he had me alone, and though I defied him with shouts, I was soon cowering under his blows.

As I think back on those early days I remember most the strained, tense atmosphere that reigned in our house—a distrust, even a fear, as if some great secret were hanging over our lives. Thinking back, it is still hard to explain. Certainly there was a stigma attached to it all in those days, whereas now there is far less. If I was illegitimate, or they thought so, they, an orthodox Jewish couple, might have wanted to protect me. But I learned much later that theirs had been an unhappy marriage before I became a part of their family—and that the addition of a child was supposed to make it better.

That never happened.

And the mystery and strain only made us less of a family.

It was always there. I kept wondering what was *wrong*, why my father seemed so cold to me, why—unlike other fathers I saw—he never wanted to hold my hand; I wondered why my old grandmother in her heavy-knit maroon shawl—a grim presence in our small apartment— kept calling me *"momser."* I didn't know until much later that the word meant "bastard." When you're a child, you have only one source for your answers: your parents. I wanted to trust them. I *wanted* to believe them—and to understand.

A child misses little.

I can remember with the greatest clarity the day I found the paper.

I was seven, and I had been playing by myself, as I usually did, sketching and cutting out dolls that I then made stands for; each little figure had its own role or part to play, and I had made six or seven that afternoon, playing beside my crib in the bedroom.

Mother had been sneezing all afternoon, and I wasn't surprised when she called in: "Florence, would you get me a handkerchief? They're in the middle drawer of the dresser."

I wanted to finish cutting out another figure but my mother called: "Florence!"

I dropped the paper doll and went to the grained walnut dresser against the wall on the other side of my crib. I yanked at the handle of the middle drawer, the one in which mother kept her linens and lingerie; it came half out and then stuck. Still thinking of my cutouts, I reached in blindly and began fishing around with my hand, making a terrible mess. I remember the sweet smell of the sachet mother kept in the dresser—and then I heard a crinkling sound and felt the stiff texture of paper against my fingers.

Quickly I pulled it out. It was a black paper with white writing on it. I'd never seen a photostat before and it frightened me. I could read very well by now, but the small white printed letters were not what caught my attention first. I saw my parents' names, Rose and Harry Ladden. I saw a strange name, Anna Fisher. And I saw the word "adopted."

Adopted? I knew that word. It meant: not *really* someone's child. It meant you were someone else's.

I left the bedroom with the paper in my hand and headed for the kitchen, where my mother was preparing dinner. My name was Florence Ladden. Who was Anna Fisher?

My mother was standing beside the refrigerator, its door slightly ajar. I saw two milk bottles inside, each with that off-white cream risen to the top. Mother had on her pink print housedress, which she frequently wore, and an apron. Her gray-white hair was set back flat on her head and tied up meticulously in a bun.

I came up close to her, holding the paper out in front of me. "Who's Anna Fisher, mommy?" I asked.

She looked startled, frightened. Her soft pink skin flushed, her eyes grew wide. She reached out quickly and tore the paper out of my hand so roughly that a piece of it ripped off. I couldn't understand what was happening. Why was she so angry? I could see it in her eyes. I could feel her body tense up and she took the paper and, without looking at it, thrust it behind her back.

"Am I Anna Fisher?" I asked her, looking deep into her eyes.

"No, no," she said quickly now. "No, there's . . . well, there's another Rose and Harry Ladden in the family. Yes. They adopted a little girl . . . and we're holding this paper for them."

I wanted to believe her. But her eyes and her voice said that something was terribly wrong. My mother was not telling me the truth.

I looked at her carefully. She had grown extremely agitated. Now and then I could see her hand, still holding the black paper, come from behind her back. Her eyes were wide. Why wouldn't she tell me the truth? There had to be some dark, awful, frightening reason. I fought back my tears. I didn't want to say it; I didn't want to accuse her. But finally I could hold back no longer:

"You're a liar!" I shouted at my mother. "You're lying to me."

I can remember how she started back. I can remember the tense twitching in her face. "You're calling your mother a liar?" she said, her voice rising. She stepped toward me and slapped me sharply on the face.

My cheek stung but now I couldn't stop. All I knew was that my mother was lying to me. "It's a lie," I shouted. "It's a lie." I looked at her eyes, which had begun to tear, and at the piece of paper in her hand. "I'm Anna Fisher," I said, fighting back my tears. "I *know* I'm Anna Fisher."

But I didn't know.

It was there but not there. For years after I found the paper, I'd wait for those times when my mother and grandmother left me alone in the apartment. As soon as the door clicked closed, I'd start to search. Systematically, I searched our entire apartment. I knew where my father kept his insurance policies and looked through every item in his packet of private papers. I looked through every inch of the dresser, many times—rummaging through all the clothes as the smell of my mother's sachet reminded me of the day I'd seen the black paper.

Anna Fisher.

The name would not leave my mind. I wrote it out on scraps of paper; I whispered it to myself; I hunted everywhere for another sight of that black paper on which I'd found it. Or had I? Had that paper really existed? I opened the seams of the upholstery of our couch, and that of the bed and the armchair—and then carefully sewed them up. I actually looked under the linoleum that covered our floors instead of carpeting. My parents must have known I was looking. They must have seen the scars of my search. But no one said a word. Now when I'd ask my mother about that name, she wouldn't even answer me. No one dropped the slightest touch of a hint, ever, that someone named Anna Fisher ever existed!

There was only one person who I knew would tell me. But I couldn't ask him.

Uncle Abe. Uncle Abe. How does a child know how and why she loves someone with her whole heart?

I loved that man with all I was. I lived for the days when he came home, and for the days when I'd visit him in the factory at which he sometimes worked or on one of the roofs on which he kept and tended his pigeons.

He was my mother's brother and slept in our living room three or four days a week, on and off, during the years we lived in New York. Sometimes he'd be gone for several months at a time, without a word, like some classic bohemian of the thirties, and I'd stand near the closet by the front door, pretending to put my Big Little books in order but really listening for the elevator that would bring him to our floor.

Mother and I sometimes went to New York City, and when Uncle Abe was working at the factory she would drop me off with him for an afternoon while she shopped in the department stores or visited a friend or relative. I'd sit for hours watching his fingers fly at his work, fascinated and deeply engrossed, and then we'd go outside together, holding hands, and he'd buy me one of the delicious hot sweet potatoes that were sold from little carts throughout the garment district.

When Uncle Abe vanished for too long a time, mother and I would go from Brooklyn to the Lower East Side and climb floor after floor of old tenements, one after the other, to look for him at one of his pigeon roosts. He and his friends kept scores of the cooing birds in wire coops on the roofs, and would often put messages on them and send the birds shuttling back and forth, delivering who-knows-what notes of cosmic import.

Then I'd suddenly see him standing beside a coop, with that straight black hair and those bright blue eyes that danced, and I'd run up to him and kiss his cheeks, burned dark from the sun of his rooftops. He had bright white teeth, and I loved to see the broad smile spread across his face. He always seemed so very happy to see me!

Often he took me for long walks in the evening, and we'd sit together on the stone bench built into the wall of the Dime Savings Bank or, if he took me to a bar, I'd sit on his knees, sip sour, sour beer, spit it out, and then we'd both laugh. Many of Uncle Abe's friends were Irish, and he sometimes got jobs as a bartender through them.

Once, when I had a bad case of the whooping cough, my birthday party had to be called off. Uncle Abe had never missed one of my birthdays, and I was upset when he didn't appear the night before. But it was Saturday, and I knew he usually came home only during the week. When I woke on Sunday morning, Uncle Abe was standing beside my crib. I remember I had on white seersucker pajamas, with a button-down flap in the back. I remember how he looked at me and, without a word, picked me up over the bars and carried me directly to the refrigerator.

He opened the door and, saying nothing, motioned for me to look inside.

There was the most enormous birthday cake I'd ever seen! It was white with pale blue topping, and it had three dark red roses on it. Beneath the roses, written in bold letters by his friend the baker, were the words:

Happy Birthday,
Florence

It never occurred to me to ask Uncle Abe about the strange paper I'd found, or about the incident concerning my birth certificate. He never once lied to me, and never, to my knowledge, lied to anyone else. It was not in his nature. No, he would not have lied about my birth certificate, or about that strange paper I'd seen, if I had asked him.

Maybe I didn't ask him because I didn't know how he'd react; it might spoil our simple, open love. Maybe I didn't ask him because I knew—and was afraid—he'd tell me the truth.

Two houses away there lived an enormous family of southern Italians. There were four or five generations of them under the same roof, and relatives always coming and going.

They'd all sit around the huge oak table in their kitchen —the old ladies wearing black stockings; the young man, Frank, playing the violin or singing; a raft of kids, racing back and forth, eating pasta all day; the marvelous old man they called simply "Nonno."

And they all looked alike! The place was absolutely lousy with people made out of the same mold.

Whenever I could I'd leave our apartment and visit them. I couldn't get enough of that family. They delighted and fascinated me. Frank saw my interest in music and began to give me free lessons on the violin. He'd hold my hand and show me how to manipulate the bow; he'd play a passage, ask me to watch, and then ask me to play it by myself. I would have preferred to learn the piano, but I was enormously grateful for any lessons I could get on any instrument; and as I grew older I knew that music would have to play an important role in my life. There was another reason, I must admit, why I took so readily to the violin. Though he was about twenty-five and I was under ten, I was madly in love with Frank.

These Italians welcomed me into their home and drew me into their songs and music. There was always music in this household. Either Caruso sang from the phonograph all day, and we all sat rapt and listening, or we sang arias ourselves from a dozen different operas—in Italian.

Nonno would often put me on his lap and let me play the piano roll. He and Frank taught me all the Neapolitan songs in Italian, and whenever I came we sang and laughed

and listened to Caruso and ate mountains of spaghetti and
then sang some more. "O Sole Mio" rang in my ears; I
could breathe in this house—my blood was awake. They
were always happy; always full of exuberance, always
laughing. What a handsome family they were—the old
great-grandfather, lean and taut and quiet; the grandfather
with his heart full of song; the old ladies with their high
black stockings, ministering to the men's needs; the adult
children with their children; and Frank, who never knew
how much I loved him. And every ear, nose, and profile
were exactly the same!

I would come from their apartment back into my own.
I would look at my mother and my grandmother, and even
at Uncle Abe. I looked like none of them. My hair was
auburn; there was no auburn in our family. I had ears
with a certain curve, a nose of a certain shape; I was small,
my mouth was large, my cheekbones were high. I looked
for this in those around me and found no correspondences.

Sometimes, at my mother's vanity table, I'd take out the
big boxes of photographs of the entire family and go
through them one by one—looking at cousins and uncles
and aunts and old grandparents in foreign clothes and
young nieces and nephews. There were three mirrors on
the table and when I arranged them properly I could look
at myself—and the pictures—from all angles at once.

At least *one* person in my mother's, or one in my
father's, family *had* to look like me. I could see their similarities to each other. I could tell that *these* two were
brothers; yes, this could well be my father's father, and
this my mother's sister. It was there. You could see it.
Some place there must be a nose, a cheek, or eyes or
ears like mine. It was such a small thing. You wouldn't
think it would hurt so much not to find one other person
in my family who looked like me.

Yes, this man's nose, I'd think excitedly—and then I'd
block off the face in sections and look only at the nose.

three times, in the three mirrors, from all angles. Or the mouth. Or this man's eyes.

Why did it hurt so much, why did I have to find some-one who looked like me?

I'd look at the photographs over and over, holding them up and turning them to the side—looking at them in the mirror next to my face, trying to find that one relative who by some facial feature would assure me that this was *my* family, that I was not an outsider. Sometimes, des-perate, I'd grasp at one and think: *Yes, I do look like him. I do. I do.*

But the next time I looked the resemblance had van-ished.

Lies are curious. If the great lie that lived in my home hurt me, condemned me to that sense of emptiness and frustration, how much more did it trap my mother. Now, when the whole drama is done, I think back on all the misery it must have caused her to maintain, over all the many years of my childhood, a lie that became a fantasy—and then a devastating mania. How it must have raged through her! It strained my mother's love for me and mine for her. She became possessive beyond belief, and no doubt terrified unto sickness that her secret would slip out.

I can remember how, when I became close to one of my girl friends in the building, she told me sharply: "I don't like that little girl and I don't want you to play with her anymore." I heard her say that hundreds of times during my childhood and adolescence; she could not seem to bear the thought of my having anyone but her.

I would insist that the girl was my friend, and that I wanted to play with her.

"You love your friend more than you love your mother," she said, with a logic I could never understand. "You're not to play with her anymore."

My mother had a pleasant voice, but as she became

more and more excited, it rose and took on a note I ha
learned to recognize—of tension and hysteria.

I said: "I will play with her."

"You love her more. You don't love your mother," sh
would say, her voice rising, taking on a sharp edge.

Time cannot dull what happened next, what happene
a dozen times in my childhood. But *why* did it have t
happen? My mother was well into her forties when I cam
to her. Is that why she was so possessive? Did she lov
me with that fierce love of a woman who has wanted ɛ
child for many, many years—and has never been able t
have one? In my mother's case, that love was no doub
aggravated by her lack of feeling toward my father an
my grandmother. Was her possessiveness rooted in a dee
fear that I might turn from her if she did not use ever
ounce of her energy to prevent it? The crib. She had kep
me supersafe in it until I was old enough and big enoug
to step out of that cage. The logical extension of that cril
was the psychological hold she put on me. My mothe
was determined to have me for herself, to share me wit
no one.

I can still hear her saying, "I'm going to kill mysel
I'm going to kill myself right now." I can still see mysel
insisting that I had a *right* to play with my friend. I'll neve
forget the first time it happened, my mother turning o
her heel and marching into the bathroom.

For a moment I heard nothing. Then she reappeared
She had something in her hand. She showed it to me an
said: "I'm going to kill myself." In her hand was m
father's straight razor.

"She's my friend," I said, my voice much lower now
"I have a right to play with her."

My mother turned back into the bathroom and slammec
the door. I heard the bolt of the door click loudly—meta
on metal.

I became absolutely quiet, trying to hold back my sobs
When she spoke again, her voice was high and thin

I'd never heard her speak like that before. Through the door she said: "When you see the blood, Florence, you'll know you've killed your mother. Killed her. Do you understand?"

I can remember how I screamed: "Please don't kill yourself!" I can still see myself lying down on the floor just outside the door. I pounded on that door. I looked at the slit of light between the floor and bottom of the door. "I'll be good," I cried. "I won't play with anyone. I won't love anybody else. Don't kill yourself. Please. I'll only love you. I promise. I promise, mommy."

There was no sound for several long moments.

I said quietly: "I'll be very good. I won't love anybody else."

Again it was silent. One. Two. Five minutes. I heard some movements behind the locked door. I wondered fearfully what she was doing.

"Mommy?" I said, in a low voice.

The lock snapped back. I never knew what I'd see. Each time I feared the worst. When she came out, I ran to her and said, over and over, "I don't love anyone but you."

After we had argued or fought, when we were both quiet, my mother would sometimes take out one or two items of jewelry from her top drawer, to look at or play with. During the height of the Depression she pawned them; I remember how she would make periodic trips to the pawnshop near Bushwick Avenue, where we'd once lived, to put down a payment or redeem a pledge. "I don't want to lose any of it," she'd say, "because someday it will all be yours." She had an engagement ring of diamonds and sapphires set in platinum; though the stones were flawed, I loved the ring. My mother used to wind a string around my finger, then put the ring on above it, and let me wear it for an afternoon. At those moments she seemed to be living for me alone. "When you're old enough," she told me, "we'll have this made smaller for you and you can always wear it."

I became an avid reader in those years between seven and ten, while we still lived in Brooklyn. I read Dumas and Hugo, *Anthony Adverse* and *Jane Eyre* several times each, *Anna Karenina* and *Wuthering Heights,* and everything and anything I could lay my hands on. But there was no privacy in the house. My grandmother occupied the living room; I was never even permitted to lock the bathroom door.

When my mother caught me behind any locked door, she'd threaten loudly until I finally came out. Thinking back, I can only assume that her concern was sexual, for I remember her insinuations well before I was ten. Once my father came into the kitchen in his underwear. My mother insisted I was staring at him and called me a little tramp. I was eight at the time. Other mothers never acted like this. Did it have anything to do with that strange name I'd seen on the piece of paper? We'd argue and then, turning, she'd mutter: "Someday I'll tell you something."

Something—that lie, that secret, whatever it was—gnawed at my mother constantly. Over the years the scenes were repeated. Only their intensity changed—growing greater, as the mystery over which she had made herself custodian took its sad toll on us all. How deeply my mother's problems must have penetrated my life—her threats to me, her jealousy of my friends and my books, her sexual fears, her dramatic threats that she would kill herself and I would be to blame.

During the day, when I had all my strength, I would put my hands on my hips and fight fiercely for what was mine, for what I thought were my rights. I felt, without ever fully knowing why, like a stranger, an outsider, a guest in that household, but this only made me tougher.

During the day.

Late in the night, lying in my crib with the bars up, I often had terrifying dreams. I'd wake, sweating and eyes wide, from the dreams. One was always the same—and it came back time after time. I had killed somebody. I don't know how, but the person was dead. That was definite. I had buried the body under a tree. In the darkness I would see a shovel, the fresh dirt, the same shadowy tree—and then I would wake trembling, my forehead wet, my hands icy, totally convinced that I had killed someone.

I knew this was impossible. I would look over to where my mother and father slept. Yes, they were both there—each on his own side of the big bed, sleeping silently night after night. I knew I couldn't have killed anyone, and the actual murder never occurred in my dream. Nor was there any indication of who I had killed. I knew only two things with surety: the body was buried beneath that tree and I was desperately afraid that someone would find me out.

Only when I was an adult and made the connection between it and my mother's saying that I was killing her, did the dream stop.

During those increasingly rare moments when my mother and I could sit down together and talk calmly to each other, she would tell me how she'd always wanted a child and how difficult her pregnancy had been.

"When I went to St. Anthony's Hospital, Florence," she'd say quietly, "the labor pains were terrible."

I'd look up sharply from my handwork. I looked into my mother's pale yellow-green eyes. She would be looking away, out the window. She was there but not there.

"The pains were simply awful, Florence," she'd say. "I had *such* a hard time when I had you."

I wanted it to be true. I wanted to believe her.

If she had labor pains, if she delivered me at St. Anthony's Hospital, she *must* be my mother.

She *was* my mother. She *was* my mother.

Then who was Anna Fisher?

Two

━━━━━━━━━━━━━━━━━━━━━━━━━━━━━━━━━━━━

I have a child. Is he the only person in the world who looks like me?

          —An adoptee

The first person I ever saw who looked like me was my son. He didn't look, as all babies do, like Winston Churchill: he looked like me. He had my eyes and my ears, and I couldn't stop looking at him. Hour after hour, I'd hold him up beside my face and we'd peer at each other in the mirror. There could be no doubt about it: *he actually looked like me.*

I had married soon after I got out of high school. Walter was as handsome as Victor Mature, and I was young and impetuous and the arguments in my home had reached epic dimensions. I had worked regularly after school in the five-and-ten and in department stores, and on Saturdays from nine to nine; but the work was dreary and held no promise, and it was all I had to look forward to. There had to be more to life, there had to be! Walter and marriage meant freedom and happiness.

My family and I had moved to Philadelphia when I was ten. There was much whispering and hushed talk about our moving. My mother flatly insisted it was impossible, she would not under any circumstances go to that city. I had never seen her resist an idea with such ferocity. My father went to Philadelphia a full year before we finally pulled up roots in Brooklyn; though he would come home every second or third weekend, I wasn't sorry to see so little of him.

My grandmother stayed in New York with one of my mother's sisters—for which I was enormously grateful—but Uncle Abe remained behind in New York, too, and I could not bear the thought of not having him near me. Unknown to the whole family, Uncle Abe had been married for a number of years, and of course would not leave his wife, Kate. A year later, when my grandmother died and we returned to New York for the funeral, the news of Uncle Abe's marriage finally came out: he had married an Irish Catholic, and the family was furious at him. For my part, a new relative was always welcome, and Aunt Kate proved over the years to be a dear, kind person and a good friend.

The mystery I had lived with as a young child was compounded in my adolescence. A child feels and senses that something is wrong, but knows that he must live with it. An adolescent rebels. It is so hard, as I think back on those years, to tell what happened without making it all sound like a case study. Much later, I could understand what was driving my mother; but while I lived through it, I could only resist her in every way possible.

In our new apartment I had a room of my own and —at last!—that crib was out of my life forever. How my friends in Brooklyn had made fun of the crib, and the fact that I was given milk from a bottle until I was seven, when I finally threw it out the window. In place of the crib, I had a junior bed, in which I slept until I was seventeen; it came replete with half sides, to keep me—my mother kept reminding me—from falling out. My new friends found a junior bed ridiculous, and were shocked that my mother didn't permit me to keep the door to my bedroom closed. The bed that at first seemed so marvelous, and which my mother kept telling me was so marvelous, was soon one of the most hateful objects in my life. Over a period of two years, I broke the slats of the sides one by one.

How different it was at my friends' houses during those years. Irene did not have to account to her mother for every minute of her time; I did. When her mother, who worked, came home in the afternoon, she would kiss Irene on the cheek, say a few pleasant words to us all, and then go about her business. I couldn't get out of our house without a third degree: "Where were you?" "Who were you with?" "Why couldn't you come home right after school?" And she read all my mail, both ways—in and out—whenever she could.

My mother seemed desperate to protect me from any harm, to protect me from the world—to protect me from myself. The last, the lack of trust or respect, hurt most.

But why? I tried, but I couldn't understand her concern. I couldn't understand her possessiveness. What was she afraid of? What, in me or about me, made her act this way?

Once, when we went back to New York for a visit, I was invited to an all-girl overnight party. I wanted more than anything to go, and couldn't see the slightest reason why I shouldn't be permitted to do so. We were staying with one of my aunts and I decided to take a shower before dressing.

"I won't permit it," my mother insisted, coming to the tub and pushing back the shower curtains.

I looked at her and fixed my jaw and said: "Please. It's going to be so much fun."

My mother became more and more determined to keep me from going.

I said: "These are my friends. What's the harm?" When she shook her head, I said: "I'm going anyway."

She stepped back for a moment, grabbed something from behind her, and then came toward me. She had a wire coat hanger in her hand. "I'll kill you," she shouted, "before I'll let you go. I'll kill you. Do you hear?"

By the time they pulled her off me, I was cut and bleeding in half a dozen places. I had tried to fight her off, but I was only fourteen—and still small and slight. I *had* to resist her; I had to fight back. Something inside me drove me to preserve—what was it?—a sense of my *rights*, yes, a sense of what stood outside of the tugging and pulling, the deception and the mystery.

For it was all, somehow, related to the mystery. I knew that it was. "Bums," "tramps," she called my friends, and I was told regularly, at fifteen, that I was bound to come home pregnant, with a big belly, and disgrace her. She told me none of the facts of life, and when I began to date the year I was fifteen, I was too shy to ask my slightly older friends. It was astounding what I didn't know about sex! That Halloween there was a big party and I made myself up elaborately, wore a cellophane hula skirt and a gay shirt covered with bright sequins that I'd made myself.

The next day I announced to my mother: "I think I got pregnant."

She put her hand on her heart and asked me what I'd done.

"I kissed Lenny three times."

"Is that all?"

"Yes," I said, hoping she'd be more impressed. Lenny was one of the handsomest boys in our group, and I was proud to have been kissed by him.

"Are you absolutely sure that's all?"

"Yes," I said.

"Well, you can't get pregnant that way."

"Then how do you get pregnant?"

She told me it was sordid and dirty and that I was not to think about it, not ever.

My mother insisted upon taking me to school every day until the ninth grade, and wanted to continue after that but I told her if she accompanied me I simply wouldn't go. Why did she act that way? Was there something about me, something mysterious and frightful, that I didn't know? She had had what, in whispers, was called a nervous breakdown when I was about seven—soon after I'd found the black paper. I wondered if I had inherited something from her—or if there was something about me, something dreadful and unspeakable about my life, which I didn't know.

Whenever I could, I'd cut school and walk twenty blocks from our home to the public library. I never told my mother where I was going, and when I came home I said I'd been playing in the schoolyard with the other girls. It was peaceful and silent in the library; I could concentrate there—and I could reread *Anna Karenina* without being told it was filthy and obscene. I had been two years ahead in school, but as the tension in my house increased, my work got poorer and poorer. For some reason, we kept moving from one apartment to another during those years—sometimes three or four times a year—and the changes were unsettling. I simply buckled under the pressure and decided to study for myself, quietly, in the library.

In school I took violin lessons for twenty-five cents each, played the violin in the school orchestra, sang with the orchestra, and also with the band, and took every course I could in sketching and painting. Since those days with the Italian family next door to us in Brooklyn, music had become tremendously important to my life; music transported me from the wasted days and the tension and the despair about my future. My parents had announced after junior high school that they would not send me to college; this troubled me all through high school. I didn't know how to go about arranging for college myself, since I was not only young but highly immature.

So I got married.

I knew after my honeymoon that I'd made a mistake—that I had married too soon, for the wrong reasons, to the wrong person for me. When I told my mother I wanted a divorce, she said: "You'll disgrace us."

Several months later, when I learned I was pregnant, I realized the dimensions of the mistake I'd made. I was no longer in love with my husband and I was not nearly ready to be a mother. But the fears went even beyond this: I began to fear for my child, what he would be, whether he would be *normal*.

Throughout my adolescence, I had buried the name Anna Fisher. I had tried to suppress it, to forget it. I never mentioned it to my mother. But when I became pregnant the name began to return at odd moments during the day and night, and I began to wonder whether I had imagined the entire episode. I rethought it, detail by detail; in my mind, I put my hand into that drawer again, smelled the sachet, drew forth the black paper, and rushed into the kitchen. I could see the off-white cream risen to the top of the milk bottle in the refrigerator. I could hear myself challenging my mother: "Am *I* Anna Fisher?"

"I'm not adopted," I began to repeat to myself. "I'll have a normal baby."

But if I *was* adopted and they hadn't told me, there must have been something terribly wrong. If I *was* adopted, who had I come from? What genes was I carrying? Were there abnormalities that might skip me but be passed onto my child? Or physical deformities? If I *was* adopted, why had I been given up for adoption? Was it because there was something wrong with my parents?

In recent years, since I have met a great number of adoptees, I have been amazed to find how many shared my fears for my baby. Is it a *rational* fear? None of the other mothers, who knew positively that they were adopted, seemed to know. But they experienced it. Fear and the unknown are inextricably linked. None of us really knew; though the other adoptee mothers recognized the *facts* of their adoptions, and perhaps even had a few bald facts about their natural parents, they didn't really know more than I, in whom the idea of adoption lived only as a vague and haunting possibility. To give birth is to establish the hereditary link. It forces you to think back about your own heritage—to think of the traits and talents, the shapes and sizes of ancestors whose genes you carry. The adoptee goes back only into himself. Beyond that there is a wall. And it is the fear of what is behind that wall— magnified a thousand rational and irrational times in one's imagination—that causes all the mischief.

I was in labor for four days. I wanted to give birth, to become a mother, and I was petrified at the thought. The labor pains began and they continued and I thought they would never stop. I kept hearing the words Anna Fisher; I imagined a hundred disasters. Deep inside I was desperately afraid of what I would produce.

When my time finally came I was given a caudal anesthetic. Throughout the delivery I was wide awake, and when the nurse pulled a gauze over my eyes I pushed it away.

"We have to do this," she said.

"No you don't. I won't stand for it," I said. "I must see my child as soon as he's born."

When they had cleaned my boy, they lifted him so I could see: he had two arms and two legs. "Is he all right?" I asked the doctor. "Is he normal?" When they brought him to me, I kept poking him gently, trying his arms and legs—looking at his face, looking into my son's eyes.

He *looked* all right. There seemed to be nothing wrong.

The first thing visitors said was: "Florence, he looks just like you!"

No words could have thrilled me more. I remembered

all those days I had searched in the faces of my relatives, and in the big boxes of family photographs, for someone who in some slight way, in any way, resembled me. There had never been another person in the world, another person I had ever seen, anywhere, who looked like me until now—and I had had to produce him myself. I picked up Glenn and held him in my arms in front of the hospital mirror. Yes. He did look like me. There could be no doubt about it. That nose, those eyes, those ears—they were my *connection* with someone outside of myself. This person was a part of me, as I must be a part of someone else, someone somewhere in the world. It was not just the eyes or the nose or the ears. I felt warm and *connected* when I looked at my little baby's face. There he was, wrapped in his soft blue blanket, with only the circle of his face showing, and that face was *my* face, and the thrill of it sent happy shivers through me. "See," I'd say to him, "Glennie looks just like mommy. Just like mommy."

Still, I watched Glenn apprehensively during his first year. He crawled on time, and began to talk, and there was quick happiness in his eyes, but he couldn't walk. He got to be ten and then eleven months. Many other children I saw were already walking. He was twelve, thirteen months old and still didn't walk. He turned fourteen months, and then he got up without holding anything, set his little bowlegs down one after the other, and took his first steps.

That same year, something happened that changed my entire relationship with my mother. She had always had migraines, but now they grew unbearable. Her anxiety increased also—and she'd clutch her head and her throat, and grow dizzy. "She needs a psychiatrist," I told my father, "not a general physician."

"What are you saying?" he shouted. "Your mother's crazy?"

I told him that she needed help badly and that she was going to get it. I could be stronger than my father now, and despite his vehement protests, I found and then took my mother to a psychiatrist, told him about the breakdown she'd once had and about the severe symptoms she now suffered. He examined her carefully for an hour and then said unequivocally that she should go to a special home for mental patients and receive shock treatment.

I had never consciously understood before this how sick my mother was.

When my mother came out of the home that spring, after extensive shock treatment, she was calmer and more rational than at any other time in my life. The treatment had calmed her hysterical possessiveness, and for the first time I saw what must have been my mother's real self. We talked frequently and often met for lunch at a downtown restaurant. She adored Glenn and was extremely kind and gentle with him. But one day while we were eating lunch in Beck's Restaurant, the fork suddenly dropped out of her hand. I watched as she lowered her arm, placed her fingers on the utensil, and then tried to pick it up. She could not lift it.

I took her out to a cab and we went to my apartment, where I insisted she stay for a few days so I could keep watch over her. The days became weeks, and I found that I genuinely enjoyed having her with me. There was much I still did not know about running a household, and I learned a great deal from her. There were none of the scenes that had become so common between us, she was glad to be away from my father, and she enjoyed staying with Glenn while I went shopping. But as the weeks wore on, she began to lose her power of movement. She had difficulty standing upright, could barely manage her arms and hands, and soon I had to feed and dress her.

Helplessly I watched as she grew more and more listless and passive. My father insisted on moving in with us and I didn't have the strength to deny him. With him, into our four-room apartment, came not only all the furniture and dishes and my mother's crystal from a five-

oom apartment, but also a constant stream of criticism
oout the way I ran my own household.

For the first time in my life I had had a real mother—
omeone I could be with and talk to, someone I could
nare my problems with. Her treatment of me had never
een caused by meanness but by some hysterical desire
nat now was stilled. Perhaps the secret meant nothing to
er anymore. I do not know. I never asked her. After all
ne years of pain and mystery, I had a mother; that and
er health were what mattered now. I wanted with all my
eart for her to get well. She had been calm these past
nonths and we had grown close.

One day she collapsed and was rushed to the hospital
ith a brain tumor. I wasn't prepared for the sight of her
n the hospital bed after her operation. "That's not my
nother!" I cried. "That couldn't be my mother." The
oman on the bed was ghostly pale. In place of my
nother's silver, wavy hair, the whole skull was tightly
andaged; this woman had no hair. I looked, hoping there
as some mistake. And there were tubes—crisscrossing
ubber tubes attached to her arms and extending past the
ed and into an elaborate apparatus.

I could not bear it. Had I found a mother only to lose
er?

Morning after morning for six weeks I went to the
ospital. My friend Raye would take Glenn, and I'd stay
ll day, go home to cook dinner for my father and hus-
and, and then return in the evening. Each day I'd go to
ny mother's bed and peer into her vacant eyes. She
carcely moved a muscle. She recognized no one except
ne anymore. Sometimes, when I approached, she'd say,
Florence. Glenn." The words were scarcely audible.

Finally a day came when I found her breathing heavily
—in spasmodic gasps. Her lips were blue. I touched her
and. It was cold.

Oh, God, I thought. *Don't let her die. Not now. Not
vhen I've just found her.* She *was* my mother. We had

shared, if only for a brief moment, a warm and tend
love.

Taking her hand lightly in my own, I said: "Mother .
mother?"

I felt her fingers close tightly around my hand. I tri
to break my hand free but could not.

"Florence. Glenn," she said.

"Yes, mother. I'm here. I'm Florence. I'm your daug
ter." I looked at her and breathed deeply. "I love yo
mother," I said softly.

And then, from the depths of somewhere, summoni
words that said there was still something inside her, s
uttered these words: "Now you'll . . . have . . . no one

She said nothing more, and when I could bear the stra
no longer, I rushed from the ward.

By the time I got home, someone at the hospital ha
phoned to say my mother was dead.

Three

―――――――――――――――――――

feel lost and floating.

—An adoptee

didn't rain until the afternoon. In the morning—it was
Sunday, November 19, 1950—the skies grew dark, the
winds grew gusty, and we all knew a devastating storm
was about to break.

My father had chosen a simple pine box; it upset me
terribly when I saw it, and I pleaded with him to bury
mother in a better coffin. "I'll pay for the difference," I
said, but he raged against any change, said it was a waste,
and this time I was in no condition to stand against him.

The simple funeral, which was held in the afternoon,
coincided with the start of the rains. First they were light,
no more than a heavy drizzle—but you could tell what
was coming. By three thirty, when we had finished and
were preparing to leave the cemetery, it was as dark as
night. The rains kept gaining strength by the minute.
Several of our black umbrellas turned up and collapsed.
The leaves were gone from the trees in the cemetery, and

the wind swayed the bare branches melancholically.

Uncle Abe had managed to come from New York, despite a broken shoulder; after the funeral I made sure that he went directly to the train station. Then, in the pelting rain, our funeral party drove from the cemetery to my home. Everyone washed their hands at the door, and then came into the living room, cluttered with all my parents' possessions from their apartment.

Before any of us were settled, several of my relatives went over to the cabinet that held all my mother's crystal. One of them, lifting a vase, said: "Well, I want *this* to remember Aunt Rosa."

"And I want this," said another, taking up a smaller vase and holding it to the light.

They had not even bothered to sit down for coffee. I knew my mother had been a second mother to these women before I was born. I knew she had been kind and thoughtful to them when we lived in Brooklyn. they loved her, why did they need her crystal to remember her by?

All evening, as one by one my relatives fingered my mother's crystal, talked about having it as a memento, and then left, my desolation grew. I felt the loss of my mother deeply, but I could not bear the thought of my father monopolizing my house all week, sitting *shiva* on wooden boxes—and I felt guilt at wanting him out. Surely he must feel grief, too—as I did, so deeply, but without the need for wooden boxes.

Finally all the family left except my Aunt Gert, one of my mother's sisters. She announced that she would stay with me and sit *shiva* with us. "I'm going to stay here a week, Florence, and help you," she said. "There will be lots to do and to decide, and you'll need my help."

Why?

She had never shown the slightest interest in me. And now, her offer to stay and care for me was completely out of character. I remembered how she had looked at a pink gold ring with little rubies that Uncle Abe had given me for my high school graduation, and said: "Your uncle, he never cares for my children; he only cares for you." Whom did Aunt Gert care for?

My father insisted that the electricity be turned off, and that we light candles. I left him with Aunt Gert, in the room with the eerie flickering lights from the candles, and went alone to the living room window. The storm was mounting now. The winds howled, the trees swayed in huge arcs. I saw the garbage can covers blown off, and heard them rattle weirdly as they flew all over the back-yard. The rain was thick now; it swept across the little yard in great slanted sheets.

My mother is out there, I thought, *all alone.* I had an image of her in that flimsy pine box. She had said that I would have no one. Whom did she have now? I started to cry softly. They had kept me insulated from the world, my mother and my father—in cribs and junior beds, by censoring my mail and censoring my friends—and I felt too young for all that was happening. I could not bear it. The storm kept growing worse, and the tempest inside me kept mounting to a terrible pitch.

I tried to sleep, but could not.

Time and again that night I went to the window and looked out at the raging storm—at the wildly bending trees and the sweeping sheets of rain.

The next morning, after I had finished serving my father and my aunt breakfast and was beginning to feed Glenn in his highchair, Aunt Gert said: "What's going to be with the jewelry?"

"What do you want?" my father asked.

I turned to look at them. In a moment they were in the middle of an animated discussion about my mother's jewelry—jewelry she had pawned for the sake of her family and then, item by item, over a period of many years, redeemed. I listened for a few moments and then lifted my son and took him into the living room.

Hour after hour their conversation droned on. "I want the pendant for Ellen and the ring for Sam. I think the hair comb is pretty. What ever happened to Rose's diamond earrings? Do you remember them?"

I came into the room and sat down, but they didn't see me. I wasn't in the room; I didn't exist for them. I walked between the two of them once, but they didn't stop talking. I served them lunch and they spoke not one word to me. I waited for someone to ask my opinion.

But I might as well not have been there.

Was this what my mother had meant when she said: "Now you'll have no one?"

Anna Fisher.

I don't remember when, exactly, I first heard that name again in my head. I had not thought about that black paper or that name since my son's birth. I had buried that name and that painful day once, and then I had buried it again. I had pushed it away, so far away that I could no longer be sure I had really found anything. Could I be absolutely sure I had not dreamed the entire episode, constructed a fantasy to explain why I didn't look like my parents, think like my parents, feel or act like my parents?

As they talked on and on, the name kept ringing in my ears.

My mother had promised me the engagement ring; she wanted me to have some of her jewelry. But I didn't care about the jewelry. Let them take everything for all I cared. I only wanted them to acknowledge my presence; I wanted them to *see* me. I wanted to scream: "I'm her daughter. What are you doing? Why don't you ask me what should be done?"

I wanted to call Uncle Abe. I didn't want to say, "Come and help me fight it out with them, they'll listen to you." I wanted to call and ask him: "Uncle Abe, why are they doing this to me?" But I didn't call. I knew Uncle Abe was ill, and I knew I would never ask him, or anyone else, to fight my battles.

The day wore on, and still that name pounded and pounded inside me, until I thought I would shout it to the world. I played with Glenn but my chest was heaving now, and I ran into the bathroom. Glenn saw me there, worn and crying, and he started to sob also.

My father shouted at Glenn to stop his confounded crying.

I could stand no more. I went to the phone and called my girl friend. "Raye," I pleaded, "please come and get me out of this house."

"What's the matter?" she asked, deeply concerned.

"They're sitting here—my aunt and my father—dividing my mother's possessions. They don't even see me. They don't see me, Raye."

She promised to come right over.

And then it hit me. If I was *really* my mother's child, my aunt wouldn't *dare* do this. *Anna Fisher*. The name was like a drumbeat in my ears. No aunt would haggle over my mother's things without consulting her daughter. No father would permit it if I was truly his only child.

Raye parked in front of the house, honked several times loudly, and I wrapped up Glenn and went out to her car. At her home, I told her everything that had happened; I spilled out all my suspicions, my fears. When she finally calmed me down, I said: "Raye, I *know* I was adopted. I can feel it. Somebody's got to tell me the truth. And they've got to tell it to me tonight."

"Who can you ask?" Raye said.

I thought for a moment, discarded a few possibilities, and then put through a long-distance phone call to a cousin-in-law on Long Island. Susan was old enough to know, for she had married into the family when I was five or six; and I believed her to be honest.

"Please tell me," I said without preamble. "I must know. Am I adopted?"

She said: "Why do you want to know?"

I told her what was happening at my apartment. I paused. "And I think I found a paper," I said tentatively. "But I'm not sure."

She said: "When do you think you found what paper?"

I spoke quickly. I couldn't wait a moment longer. "I was seven. I saw a name—Anna Fisher—and . . . and, oh, for God's sake, tell me. Tell me, Sue. I can't stand it anymore. My son is almost two and a half. I'm not a baby. I have a *right* to know."

The receiver was dead for a long few moments; I pressed it closer to my ear. "Yes, you found the paper."

I closed my eyes and let out an enormous breath. I looked over at Raye and nodded my head.

"Florence? Are you there?" Susan said.

I breathed deeply again. "Yes. Yes, I'm here. It's all right."

"Are you sure?"

"Of course," I said. "What else do you know?"

"Well, when you found the paper," Susan went on, "your mother destroyed everything—every one of the papers. I begged her to tell you, but she refused. She said she'd kill anyone in the family who told you."

"No, no," I said quietly.

"She swore everybody to secrecy, Florence, and thought that if she destroyed the papers you'd never know. You were only a child; you'd forget having seen anything."

All those years. All those long lonely years—thinking of that paper, dreaming of it. Now I knew. And knowing was so different from thinking and dreaming. I had felt *something*. I had tried to bury the name Anna Fisher, but now it was back. I had found a mother—and lost her. There was nothing now. Only limbo. I was *nobody's* child.

"Florence, are you there? Are you still there, Florence?"

I asked in a flat voice: "Who was my mother? Who was my father?"

Susan didn't know. She thought she'd heard that he

was a law student or a lawyer, and she remembered being told that my mother was a teacher. She didn't know their names. They might have come from Philadelphia, she told me, because when my father's firm moved from New York my mother didn't want to go for fear she'd meet my real mother some day on the street.

"Is that all, Sue? Don't you know any more?"

"I know the adoption was why you moved so often when you were a teen-ager. She'd tell someone in the neighborhood and then develop a terrible fear of that person telling you."

"Oh, my God!"

"I don't know anything else, Florence, and I'm afraid no one else does, either. She was terribly secretive about it all."

When I got off the phone I immediately began to wrack my brain for any hint of how I could learn more. That night. I had to learn *that* night who I was, who my parents were. I had lived with lies and mysteries long enough.

I didn't want to call Uncle Abe. He would have known something, but I didn't want him to know I *wanted* to know. It would only hurt him. After a few moments I said to Raye: "When we lived in New York, a Dr. Green took care of me. Green. Green. Alvin P. Green."

I called New York information; there *was* a Dr. Alvin P. Green in Brooklyn. I scribbled down his address and phone number, hung up, and dialed the number. A man answered.

"Dr. Green?" I said.

"Yes," he said cautiously.

"I don't know if you'll remember me but you took care of me when I was a little girl. My name is Florence Ladden and . . ."

"Oh," he said. "You mean the adopted child?"

The adopted child. I couldn't keep from crying, and he must have heard my sobs as I said, haltingly, "I just found out."

He said: "I thought they told you."

"They never told me," I said. "Dr. Green, do you know *anything* about me? Who my mother was?"

"I delivered you," he said flatly.

"If you delivered me," I said, my excitement rising, "then . . . then you must know my real mother."

"Why do you want to know?"

"My mother just died," I said, "and now I find she wasn't my real mother. I'm confused. I don't know who I am." The questions came tumbling out: "If you delivered me, you *must* know all about me. Who was my mother? What's her name? Where is she?" I couldn't stop; suddenly a thousand questions swirled in my brain. "Who was my father? What did my mother look like? Please tell me what she looked like. Please tell me *something* about her."

Sitting in my friend Raye's home, talking to the best possible person to answer my questions, I saw a way to fill the great emptiness that had been growing for so long. Before it had been a dark shadow; now it was real; now I *knew*. And this man, I thought, has all the answers.

His reply came in flat, belligerent tones: "I'm not going to tell you anything. This isn't any concern of yours. It's none of your business."

"None . . ."

"You have absolutely no right to this information."

Angry and hurt, crying now, and full of a fierce desire to know, I said: *"Right?* It's me. It's my life. Of course I have a right to know. I have a child . . . I'm a grown woman. I have the best right in the world to know. Can't you understand, Dr. Green?"

He could not. He was adamant in his refusal to help me. He only admitted that, in a "gray-market deal," he had arranged the adoption. Both women had been his patients: one because she could not become pregnant, the other for prenatal care. When I told him that I was going to come to New York to see him, that I *had* to know, he said, "Under no circumstances, young woman, will I help you or give you any further information whatsoever."

"Please let me have an appointment," I pleaded. "You must give me this information."

"Must?"

"You brought me into the world, Dr. Green. You have an obligation to me as a human being. I have a right to know and you *must* tell me."

He said: "I certainly don't intend to."

"I'm coming anyway," I said.

"Don't bother," he said, "I won't see you." He hung up the receiver. The sound slammed into my ear.

Later, Walter came to pick me up. We had grown further apart. We were only technically married now. When we were in the car, he asked why the devil I'd left home, left my father and my aunt alone at a time like this, to visit a friend I could see anytime.

I told him about my father and Aunt Gert and the jewelry, and then I told him what I had found out from Susan and how nasty Dr. Green had been.

"So?" he said.

"Don't you understand?" I asked, looking over at him in the dark car. "I have to find out."

"What difference does it make?"

I watched the rain beating against the front window as the car wove through the leaf-plastered streets. "It makes all the difference," I said slowly, "to me."

He launched into an animated lecture. He told me how ungrateful I was, that my parents had taken me out of the gutter, wiped my nose, diapered me. My obligation was to them. He said I was desecrating my mother's name by even thinking of going to look for my real mother. And during the week I should be mourning, sitting *shiva!* I should be ashamed.

All week, while my father and my Aunt Gert haggled over what was to be done with my mother's belongings, the fact of my adoption haunted me. It explained so much, but what did it mean? I wanted to know the facts, all of them—who I was, who I came from. Walter's harsh words kept coming back to me. Was I *really* ungrateful? What difference *did* it make? Was it merely idle curiosity or something more? What should I do?

By Thursday, I decided that I could not bury my search. Once before I had searched for the meaning of the name Anna Fisher; this time, no matter how long it took, I would not abandon that search until I found answers. This time I would not be searching under linoleum and inside up-holstery. I had seen a portent in Dr. Green of what was to come; there might be a hundred Dr. Greens, but some-where there was a person or a piece of paper that would tell me what I wanted to know. Perhaps even Dr. Green himself. He would *have* to see me. I knew I had to start with him.

2

The Search

Four

It seems when you say "adoption" everyone just clams up completely.

—An adoptee

Adoptees, when they learn they are adopted or when they become adults, all share two questions: "Should I look?" and "How should I look?"

Many are reluctant to undertake what I now know is called by them all, "The Search." They fear hurting their adoptive parents, whom they may love deeply, or feel deep gratitude toward; somehow the search, to so many people, signifies ingratitude and rejection. Already I feared Uncle Abe would be hurt if I looked for or even showed interest in my natural parents.

Many think about the difficulties a long search will entail, the years it may take, the time stolen from their family lives or work or leisure, the unsettling of what, by law, seems already to have been settled.

Some fear what they'll find out. Others simply don't care to find out anything.

But I cared. At first I may not have known why, but about the fact of looking I had no doubts: I had to look. There was something about me that I didn't know. There was a secret that had stained my childhood. No, I scarcely considered the first question when I found out I was adopted. I didn't trouble myself for a moment about *whether* I should look, only how.

Yes, how?

More than twenty years had passed since my birth and I wanted to find out . . . find out *what?* Well, something. Anything. Some scrap of information about something that had happened more than twenty years earlier, some place, between two people who happened to have been my natural parents. I was looking for a little light. Light that might lead me back twenty years. To what? To my origins, to my history. To two people, perhaps. To something called the truth. Twenty years was a long time, but already I'd been lucky; I had the name of a man who knew my natural parents, or at least my mother, and who had delivered me.

I had a name, Anna Fisher, but I didn't know if it was real. I had seen it only once, for a few moments, when I was seven years old.

My parents might be named Fisher. A common name. They might not be.

They might live in New York or Philadelphia—or Kalamazoo. They might be dead.

I was neither a tracer of missing persons nor lost parents; I was a woman in her early twenties, with a child and a mystery. I was small and sensitive, but I knew I could be strong-willed. I didn't like to push, but I knew I could. But where could I begin? How should I start?

How would *you* begin to look for two people who, twenty years earlier, had conceived you, for a mother who had given birth to you—some place; whose names you didn't know? Who might have been anyone, anywhere, except they weren't; they were your *parents*. Where would *you* start?

I took a wild chance.

Early the next week, I called the New York City Board of Health and asked them where I should write for a copy of my birth certificate. I knew my birth date. I trusted my memory of the name Anna Fisher, and I remembered that my mother had told me about her labor and delivery in St. Anthony's Hospital. I was told to write to the Bureau of Vital Statistics in Brooklyn. I did so, signing the letter "Anna Fisher."

Two weeks later, I plucked the official envelope out of my mailbox. It seemed so thin that at first I thought, as I tore it open, *There's nothing inside.* But when I turned the envelope upside down and ruffled it, out fell a photostat—a black paper with white writing on it.

My immediate reaction was disappointment. *This* was not the paper I had found in the middle drawer of my mother's dresser fifteen years earlier. This paper was smaller than the one I remembered—and narrower. This one did not mention Rose and Harry Ladden, and it only referred to a "Baby Fisher." But there was other information that I could add to my slowly growing store of knowledge about my origins. The paper read:

BABY FISHER
Mother: Florence Cohen
Father: Frederick Fisher
Father's Occupation: clerk
Mother's Occupation: housewife
Mother's Married Name: Florence Fisher

My mother's address was listed as 695 Broadway, in Brooklyn. I remembered that Susan had said my father was a lawyer or law student, and that my mother was a teacher. No matter. This had to be my real birth certificate: the date and the hospital were the same, and the name

Fisher, I was positive, was that which I'd seen when I was seven. Just like that—"Fisher," without the *c*. I had hoped this would be the paper I remembered, but it was something solid and I treasured it. In a curious way and at that time, it was confirmation to me that I really existed.

On Friday, December 22, in a blizzard, Raye and I drove to New York. The next morning I called Dr. Green's office, not to make an appointment but to learn his office hours. Then, dressed in a red suit and black sweater, and with a leopard muff I'd made myself, I went with Raye to see the man who could, if he wanted to, tell me what I needed to know.

The door was open and we walked directly into the drab empty waiting room. There was no nurse, so we sat together on the reception couch for ten minutes, saying practically nothing to each other, looking at the dirty beige walls and fidgeting with a magazine or two that we took from the round lamp table. When the door to the doctor's private office opened, my eyes snapped toward it. A medium-sized man in a white smock—about sixty, with a slight moustache and thin-rimmed glasses—walked out with a patient, said a few words to her, and then turned to us. When he saw me, his head jerked and he gave a short gasp.

When his patient left, I stood up, walked toward him, and said: "I'm Florence Ladden."

"Yes," he said.

Did he know me? Why had he seemed so startled, as if he'd seen someone he thought long dead?

He was obviously irritated, even angry, and asked what I wanted. But he was my main lead; I had no choice but to pressure him.

"I'd like to talk to you," I said. "I've come all the way from Philadelphia."

Then, as I walked past him and into his office, uninvited, he said: "I told you not to come."

I sat down without saying a word, pulled my muff onto

my lap, opened it, and took out my birth certificate. Like a little girl reciting in class, I held it out and said rapidly: "Here's my birth certificate. I didn't have this when I called you. Florence Cohen is my mother and Frederick Fisher is my father. I got my birth certificate and now I know everything." I carefully placed the paper on the desk in front of him; it was the most precious possession I'd ever had. I was sure he'd talk to me now.

Dr. Green took the paper and, scarcely glancing at it, flipped it roughly across his desk. It fell off the other side. "You shouldn't have that," he said.

I jumped to retrieve it, and held it out again. "See," I said, insistently, "it says so right here. Florence Cohen is my mother and Frederick Fisher is my father."

"Frederick Fisher was not your father," he said coarsely, waving the paper aside. "You never had a father. Your mother lied. There never was a Frederick Fisher. What makes you think there was?"

"It says here," I said, hearing my voice grow thin and pitched, "that Frederick Fisher . . ."

"He wasn't your father. What else do you want to know? Didn't you have a good home? Aren't you grateful? The Laddens took you in when no one else wanted you. Can't you understand, you're illegitimate. You had no father."

I began to choke up, but I persisted in my questions. He told me—his voice sharp and full of venom—"So what if they didn't tell you? Maybe they did it for your sake? What can be gained by all this? I don't know where your mother is and if I did I wouldn't tell you."

The past months had been devastating for me. I had come to this man for some compassion. I needed someone to put his arms around me and tell me, "Florence, it's all right." Dr. Green said: "You're illegitimate. Is that what you want to know? Now are you satisfied?"

I pleaded with him, but his tone only became more belligerent. I knew he knew more. Why, why wouldn't

he tell me? What could it mean to him? I was a grown
woman. I was entitled to the information I sought.

At last, his tone brusque, he said: "Look, don't bother
me. Get out of here." He took me by the arm, led me past
Raye to the door, and said: "Get out. And don't come
back."

Raye returned to Philadelphia on Sunday, promising to
take care of Glenn for me for a few days. I couldn't return.
Dr. Green's rebuffs, instead of turning me away, had only
whetted my desire to press further in my search. The birth
certificate had mentioned 695 Broadway as my mother's
address at the time of my birth. Early on Monday, I headed
for Brooklyn. It was Christmas Day.

My plan was to go to every apartment in the building,
to find someone who had lived there for more than twenty
years, and to get whatever scrap of information I could
about Florence Cohen, Florence Fisher and Frederick
Fisher. I doubted if any relative of mine still lived in
the building; but there was always the slim chance—and
certainly a better chance that someone would remember
the name.

I brought with me a stenographer's spiral notebook
and marked down the apartment number of every doorbell
I rang. Door to door I went. "My mother once lived in
this building," I said, and trotted out my birth certificate
and showed it to the person at the door. "I just found
out I was adopted," I said over and over. "Have you lived
in the building for more than twenty years?" Several people
had lived there that long, but not one remembered a family
with either name, Cohen or Fisher.

What a lonely Christmas Day it was, and how desolate
I felt checking off apartments, one by one in my notebook,
saying that I was looking for my mother so often that I
began to choke and cry on the words. I went back the
next morning, to check out the apartments at which there
had been no one home. No one remembered anyone by

he name of Cohen or Fisher ever having lived at 695
Broadway.

I returned to New York several weekends, wandered
hrough the neighborhood that surrounded 695 Broadway,
and asked various shopkeepers if they knew my mother.

On January 12, 1951—a Friday—I returned to New
York again, this time intent on visiting the place of my
birth, St. Anthony's Hospital. The hospital, I knew, would
have had to keep complete records. I asked the nurse at
he information desk if I could please see the mother
superior or nurse-in-charge, and was led a few minutes
ater into a nearby room and introduced to a nun sitting
behind a small desk.

"I was born here," I said, when I was seated. The nun
miled warmly at me. "Here's my birth certificate. I'm
adopted."

The smile froze and a frown veiled her face.

"I'm looking for my mother," I said. "I'm sure you
have complete records here, because when I gave birth
o my son, the hospital took down all . . ."

"I'm terribly sorry," she said, interrupting me. "There's
nothing we can do for you."

The people at 695 Broadway had not been hostile; they
imply did not have the information I needed. Dr. Green
new, but for some reason he wouldn't tell me. Now, at
his hospital, the facts of my origins might be in one of
hose filing cabinets, or even in this woman's desk. She
ad to let me see the papers.

She asked me about my adoptive home. "Don't you
eel that your obligations are to your adoptive parents?
Don't you owe your loyalty to the people who took you,
aised you, fed you, cared for you?" She asked me to think
f what might have happened to me had they *not* taken me
1. "Dwell," she said, "on your proper obligations. Dwell on
he fact that you should be eternally grateful, and on the
errible fate that would surely have befallen you had these
ood people not taken you into their home."

I looked at the cross that hung from the nun's neck—a heavy cross, heavily gilded with silver ornamentation—and the chains that swept around her white cassock. I pleaded with her to let me have what I wanted, that I had come all the way from Philadelphia and that I had a child of my own and that I had a *right* to know.

"I find myself at a great loss," she said, in measured tones, "to understand this idle curiosity."

Idle curiosity? "I *must* find out who I am," I insisted.

"What you are is not a product of what your natural parents were. You are what your adoptive parents made you."

I begged her to reconsider.

"There is nothing we can do for you. The records are private." She stood and indicated that I was to leave. "I have no more time to discuss such matters," she said.

I rose, caught a touch of the antiseptic hospital smell in the room, and turned to walk out. As I did, she said: "I would appreciate it if you did not return."

I left St. Anthony's in a daze. Would it always be like that? Would everyone I saw say what Dr. Green and the nun had said? I had tried to press both of them—and I had held back a great emotional scream inside me that wanted to press them still further. I had such few sources—the doctor, the hospital, an address, several very common names. Each one was precious. I could not afford to let another go by without being absolutely sure I had done everything in my power, however unpleasant it might be, to get the information that was available. One of these sources might actually be the only one with valid facts. If I gave up too easily I might lose my only chance.

I had planned one more stop that trip—to the Surrogate's Court in Brooklyn. I had no knowledge of the law surrounding adoptions, but if there had been a legal paper in my adoptive parents' possession, that same paper must be on file in the district in which the adoption took place.

It was a raw day and I wandered aimlessly for a half

hour and then decided to go directly by subway, without eating lunch, to the Surrogate's Court. I only had a day free, and I wanted to cram as much into it as possible.

"May I see the adoption records, please?" I asked one of the clerks in the Hall of Records.

"Of course," he said casually. "They're in those huge ledgers. Find the year you're looking for, and then take the ledger to one of the tables."

I had come into the huge old hall furtively. I had expected resistance. There was none.

Using my birth certificate as a guide, I went through several of the large old ledgers with heavy bindings. There it was: my Order of Adoption. I felt a shiver of excitement when I saw it. There was that name, "Anna Fisher," and my adoptive parents' names. I read rapidly, starved for any new scrap of information I could find out about myself. "An investigation having been made by George D. Usk," it read. *Yes*. ". . . with the consent of Florence Fisher and Frederick Fisher," the court felt the welfare of Anna Fisher would be improved by this adoption. On the back of the document there was an attorney's name, Milton Wax, and his address; he had drawn up the petition to the court on behalf of the adoptive parents.

I felt enormously happy. But *this* was not the paper I had found when I was seven. This paper was long; the one I'd seen so long ago had been shorter, and I remembered that some lines had been drawn across it. This one had no lines. *Where is the other paper? Would it be here, too, in this building?*

But I was too overjoyed to think further about the discrepancy. I closed the ledgers, put them back on their shelves, and had photostats made of both sides of the document. Then, noting the midtown address of the lawyer, Milton Wax, I hurried from the building. If he was the lawyer who had handled my adoption, he would have known my mother and—if I really had one—my father. I couldn't wait to get uptown.

The office was small and drab, and the receptionist said that Mr. Wax was out. "Do you have an appointment?" she asked.

"No. But I'll wait. I must see Mr. Wax this afternoon."

I sat tensely on a chair in the little waiting room, looking up each time the phone rang.

"Mr. Wax," I heard the secretary say into the phone, "there's somebody waiting to see you." He must have said, "Let me speak to her," for a minute later the secretary motioned for me to come over to her desk and take the receiver.

I took a deep breath and said: "Mr. Wax, this is Florence Ladden. I understand you arranged my adoption. I've just come from the Surrogate's Court where I got my Order of Adoption and . . ."

"You're not supposed to have that!" he barked.

I said: "You arranged my adoption. I'd like to talk to you about it if I can." I paused for a moment and then added: "I just found out I was adopted and it's extremely important for me to know . . . to find out . . . anything you can tell me about my mother."

He said: "I can't give you any information."

"Please tell me something!"

"You have no right to any information whatsoever," he said sharply. "You were adopted legally, your name is Florence Ladden; Rose and Harry Ladden were your parents. You had no other parents."

"I had two other parents," I said quietly. "Florence Cohen and Frederick Fisher."

I heard him take a heavy breath—a kind of impatient sigh; and then he told me abruptly that he didn't want to see me, that he was not coming back to his office that afternoon, and that I should not return.

I turned the phone over to the secretary and she looked at me and nodded while she listened to what Mr. Wax had to say. I went downstairs, dejected, lonely, helpless. I drank a cup of coffee, walked over to Bryant Park, and then went into the New York Public Library. I loved libraries and often went to one when I was upset or when I wanted to be alone.

But when I got inside, I could not sit still. I could think of nothing but the photostats I'd obtained at the Hall of Records, and the names I'd now seen for the second time on an official document. I took the paper out, looked carefully at it, and read it through again. Why hadn't I thought of the obvious? I went to the current telephone directories.

Was it possible that I could simply pick up the phone and speak to one of my parents?

There were hundreds of Fishers and perhaps thousands of Cohens. *Where should I begin?* I laid all the nickels I had in my purse on the shelf near the telephone, and called five or six "F" or "Frederick" Fishers first. Nothing. None of them remotely fit the man I was looking for, nor did they know *my* Frederick Fisher.

I felt sure that Wax would be coming back to his office, but decided to make more calls before returning there; distasteful as I found it to turn up where I wasn't wanted, I was positive I could get to see him before the afternoon was over. I looked at the lists of names, shrugged, and then began following the columns of tiny type, name by name, from the *A* to *Z* of the first names of Fisher and Cohen. *What am I looking for?* I didn't know. I was grasping blindly at straws. I was desperate and I knew of no other way to search. I had to do something. I went through the Brooklyn, Manhattan, and Bronx phone books first slowly, then race-horsing through the list. *Is there a Frederick Fisher?* I kept asking myself. Dr. Green had said the name was a lie. He had said I was illegitimate. The further I went, the more ambiguous it all became.

I got more nickels. I placed them in a small pile on the phone shelf. *If I'm determined, and call them all, I* thought, blindly, *maybe someone will know, maybe someone will give me a clue.*

It was late in the afternoon when I finished and set off for Wax's office. Maybe he would tell me something, anything. It was worth a try.

I had eaten practically nothing all day, I had traveled downtown and uptown, and I now walked slowly back to his office. By the time I got there I was shaking violently. I straightened my hair at the door, pulled some of the rumples out of my clothes, mustered all the remaining strength I had—which was little enough—and walked in. I was tired and I was scared. I felt like a little girl begging for a favor.

"Is Mr. Wax back?" I asked the secretary.

"Yes," she said, answering quickly, without a thought—and then remembering.

"Would you please tell him that Florence Ladden has come back and that I'd like to see him."

Without a word to me, she buzzed the intercom, reported that I was in the outer office, paused, and then told me to speak into the box.

I said: "Look, Mr. Wax, I know you're an attorney. I know you have to keep things in confidence. I understand this. If you feel that you really can't give me all the information I want, I'll understand. But please," I said, "please just open up the door and tell me if I look like my mother."

He flatly refused.

"Who will it hurt?" I pleaded. "Can't you just take a look at me? Can't you tell me, was she short? Was she tall? Was she dark? Did we have the same ears or eyes or nose? Just look at my face. Please. Please just tell me if I look like her." Always it came back to appearances. *Why should it matter if I look like someone else,* I thought. But it did matter: it was a connection.

"I will not tell you anything whatsoever. You have absolutely no right to any information . . ."

Please, I thought. *Say something kind. Don't close the door like this.*

"Weren't your parents good to you?" he asked.

That question again. For the third time—the intimation that I should be eternally grateful, and therefore my quest was ridiculous and irrelevant. Why couldn't they disconnect the two issues? Even if my adoptive parents had been good to me that had nothing whatsoever to do with my desire to make some connection with my natural parents. Why couldn't they understand? Why couldn't anyone understand?

I heard him saying, "Please don't disturb me again. Ever."

He wanted me out, as soon as possible. *Little problem go away, don't come back another day.*

I began to cry. I couldn't leave without trying harder. I begged him again: "Please, please, Mr. Wax. Won't you help me?"

He said: "I have nothing else to say to you." The intercom went dead.

It was dark outside when I left the building. I felt worn, drained, frustrated, and confused. What were *my* rights? Why did they all turn away? I clenched my fists. *He had no right,* I thought, *to refuse me so little. What difference could it make to him?* I wanted to return immediately, to go boldly up to that closed door, open it, and confront the man directly. But I was too young—and too shattered.

I remember going into Dubois Cosmetics to buy some lipstick and a compact. Somewhere during this long day, at St. Anthony's, at the Surrogate's Court, at the lawyer's office, or at the library, I had lost my cosmetics case.

I wandered aimlessly up and down Fifth Avenue for a half hour, and then, unable to stop the compulsion that had driven me all day, I took the subway out to Williamsburg. It was evening now, and cold and dark, but I had to go back to 695 Broadway, the house where—perhaps—it had all begun. I looked at the old building for a long time but did not go in. And then I wandered, as I would do countless times during the next years, throughout the

neighborhood, past the old shops, beneath the black e
I promised myself I would return and go through th
entire area if necessary, brick by brick by brick.

When I returned to Philadelphia, I felt a great sens
of removal from everything—a tremendous loneliness tha
welled up out of some deep longing inside me. I felt empty
I moved in a haze. I couldn't concentrate on anyone o
anything. My husband continued to berate me for con
tinuing my "adolescent search."

What was I longing for? A mother? A father? I don'
think so. I was young and I was hurt. I had suddenly bee
thrust into another world, one in which I had anothe
mother and father whom I wanted desperately to know
one which vitiated a lifetime of lies and deception, an
half-explained and half-muddied what I knew about my
self. Would it have made any difference if I'd been tol
I was adopted years earlier—perhaps on the day I'd firs
found the paper that still remained so vivid in my brain
Few adoptive parents told children they were adopted i
those days; mine, in that respect, had not been so unusual
I do not think that telling me would have done more tha
remove the shock and despair I had felt, finding out a
I had. I don't think I would have felt less urgency to seel
out my natural parents. They held answers; there wer
things about myself that I felt I could only know b
knowing them: mannerisms, habits of thought, desires
character traits. If I could only find my roots, if I coul
only break through the horrible veil of the unknown.

It became an obsession. If I saw someone on the stree
who looked like me, I'd turn and follow her. If someon
idly said to me, "You look like someone I know," I fel
I had to pursue it further. I'd tell her I was adopted an
that I didn't know who I looked like, I didn't know wh
my parents were. Maybe I have a sister; maybe I have
mother or father somewhere. "Is it possible you've see
one of them?" I'd ask that person's age, and what, pre

cisely, they looked like and where they lived. The more questions I asked, the less cooperative the person became.

What a curious, naïve, and compulsive pattern this was —and yet I have in the past year and a half received hundreds of letters from adoptees who do exactly the same thing. When you begin The Search, no holds are barred: you pass up no chance, however remote. You cannot afford to.

As the months went on, I realized that I had little enough third-hand information—and had been denied what little more I sought. But I did not really want facts from a doctor or a lawyer or a hospital. The facts of my natural parents' lives, I realized, were only preliminary concerns. I wanted to look at them, touch them, talk to them. What I wanted I had to get from them personally. There was— how can I put it?—an emptiness, a longing in my heart that only they themselves could fill. I wanted to *know* them, if only for ten minutes.

I spoke to Susan several times, seeking more leads. After that first revelation, she usually tried to put me off. It was "degrading" to my mother's memory, she insisted, to pursue this matter any further. I had found out I was adopted—wasn't that enough? "How can you do this thing?" she asked. But I always kept questioning her. Once she reiterated that she thought my parents had come from Philadelphia; she wasn't sure, but it was a possibility. Another "perhaps." Another fragment—true or untrue. I had forgotten that she'd mentioned it the night she'd first told me I was adopted.

I cherished the fragment. I added it to my ever-so-slowly growing store of possibilities.

Well, I thought, as long as I'm in Philadelphia, I'll do what I can here. So I called every Cohen in the Philadelphia phone book. There were fewer than in New York, but even so the job took several days. When I finished, I tried the Fishers. All of them.

Name after name proved unfruitful; I checked off each

in the phone directory and then tried the next. About half-
way through the list, a woman answered and said: "Why
do you want to find Frederick Fisher?"

I detected a slight southern accent, and a wariness I'd
learned to recognize.

"Why do you want to find Frederick Fisher?" the
woman repeated.

I struggled to maintain my calm. I said quickly: "He's
my father. I was given up for adoption." I had not mentioned my adoption when I called the Cohens. It was
easier to say, "He's my father" than "She's my mother";
the onus is rarely on the man.

The woman said bluntly: "I can't help you."

I said: "Why did you ask me why I wanted to know
if you don't know him?"

She mumbled something I didn't hear. Her voice was
more than wary now; it was downright antagonistic.

"Please," I said, "don't hang up on me. If you know
my father, or you know where he is, please take my number and then if he wants to contact me he can do so.
My number is . . ."

She said: "I can't be bothered." I heard the phone click.

I called her right back, but when she heard my voice
she hung up immediately. She hung up on me three more
times in the next two days, without telling me a thing,
without taking my name or number—twice when she
heard my voice.

I knew this woman was lying. I could have sworn by
my life that she knew a Frederick Fisher. Twenty years
later, I learned that I was right—that her lie had effectively
cost my father and me twenty years of our lives.

Five

*A major part of my life has been characterized by
rejection. Now I am married with a child of my own
and although I have found happiness through my own
family, I will never be at peace within myself until
I find my natural parents.*

—An adoptee

It is now more than twenty years since I left Philadelphia
and returned to New York. They have been years full of
challenge and growth. I had always wanted to fill my life
with the things I loved—music, theater, and good books—
and while I was by now fully determined to see my search
through, I was also determined not to let it destroy me.
I wanted to use all my energies and talents productively;
I wanted to survive as a human being.

In May, one year and a half after my mother had died
and I had learned of my adoption, I returned to New York.
Lack of communication between my husband and me, and
my immaturity when I married, had created a gap that had
now widened to the point where prolonging my marriage
was impossible.

75

When I remarried several years later, one of the first things my husband, Stan, and I did—when we could afford it—was to buy an old upright piano. I began, with the greatest delight, to take piano lessons. I had always been able to play by ear, and I could still play the violin quite well, but I wanted now to make up for all those years when I hadn't had the opportunity to study music.

I had begun to work for a law firm as a legal secretary, and yet found time several days a week to attend music school. Where before I had always had trouble concentrating or disciplining myself, I now forced myself to concentrate on my music, which had always been such a deep love, and soon had mastered scales and chords, the beginners' lessons, and had moved on to Bach and Chopin.

I had a hunger not to let life pass me by. I wanted my new marriage to be good and my life full.

I continued to read constantly, expanding my interests to Sigrid Undset, Kafka, and Dostoyevsky; I took lessons in Afro-Cuban dancing at Katherine Dunham's, taught myself Spanish and Italian, and kept making a variety of crafts objects—handbags with purple plumes, hats with veils and flowers and bells. I had always loved Italian music and still remembered many Neapolitan songs I'd learned at the apartment of that marvelous Italian family in Brooklyn. If I'd had my choice of cultural heritages, I would have opted for being Italian.

I went to the opera several times a week in season, and I especially loved *Turandot* and, best, the towering *Otello*. I would have loved to be an entertainer, to have sung in Broadway musical comedies; but if it was too late for that, I could still take singing lessons, I could still enjoy the best music New York had to offer, and I could sing—constantly, ecstatically, in English, Spanish, and Italian—in my own home.

While I was making my life in New York, my adoptive father had remarried in Philadelphia. The jewelry that

ad been so haggled over, and which had precipitated my
all to Susan the day after my mother's funeral, went to
is second wife. All I was given—and only after I
leaded for them—were my mother's wedding band and
he engagement ring I'd always cherished—neither of
hich my father valued. I must still have wanted *some*
onnection with this man, for I returned to Philadelphia
everal times to see him, once during a snow storm.

When my stepmother died, I returned for the funeral.
he was buried fifteen feet from my mother, in a cemetery
r from the city. Though by now I had turned away from
ligion, I had a strong impulse to perform the traditional
ewish rite of putting a little stone on the gravestone of
y mother, to show I had been there and remembered
er. After the funeral service was over, I told my father
hat I was going to do.

He said: "I don't want you to."

"Why?" I asked. "You were married to her for thirty-
ine years."

"Because I said so." The words brought back in a rush
l the days when he'd cut off discussion with that phrase:
ecause I said so.

Well, not this time, I thought.

"I don't want you to do it," he continued hoarsely. "If
ou go, I'm going to leave you here."

Leaving me was inconceivable. It was midwinter, the
round was frozen, and it was late in the day; there was
o transportation from the cemetery to the city. I shook
y head sadly and walked over to my mother's grave-
one. There I bent down, picked at a few stones in the
ozen earth, found one I liked, and placed it on the top
f the simple marble marker. I stood there for a moment,
emembering our last months together, and the pine box,
nd the November storm, and that incessant talk about
er jewelry.

When I turned back, I saw my father and his wife's
amily getting into their cars. I stood watching as the

motors turned over and the cars disappeared slowly into the half darkness.

There was not another car, not another person in sight. *They'll wait for me at the gate,* I thought. *They can't just leave me here.*

Soon I was lost. All the plots looked the same; everywhere I turned there were gravestones—little headstones, large gravestones, family monuments. It was dark now and I could only stumble along, half frozen, from one plot to the next, hoping I was going in the direction of the gate.

When I finally got to the gatehouse about an hour later, the caretaker, shocked to see someone wander out of the cemetery after dark, told me the funeral party had long since departed. He was good enough to call someone with a car. By the time I returned to New York it was late at night and I was shivering and bone-tired.

I must have wanted a father sorely—for sometime later, I invited him to stay with us in New York for several days. He was a dour, unpleasant guest, constantly complaining. He became especially acrimonious when I asked him about my adoption. I had done so several times before, but he had only grunted and said he knew nothing about it.

He was sitting on our turquoise couch one evening when I said to him: "Look, dad, I know I'm adopted. I have the papers."

"What do you mean?" he asked.

"I have the papers—my birth certificate and my Order of Adoption."

"I don't know what you mean."

I went into the bedroom and brought out the copies of those two documents. I laid them in front of him.

He turned his head away and said: "I don't know what you're talking about."

"Of course you know what these papers are," I insisted. "You adopted me. You can't deny it, can you?"

He grunted. "I'm not going to talk about it."

"Won't you tell me *anything?*" I asked. Why was he so

ncredibly reluctant to say something positive about this event that was so central to both our lives?

"Why can't you even admit that you adopted me?" I asked.

He got up and left the room.

Two days after he left I went looking for the documents. They were nowhere to be found. I searched every corner of our small apartment—every drawer, every closet, every inch of our three rooms. I called my father n Philadelphia. He admitted nothing. He said he knew nothing about any papers.

When my father died some years later, I could not bring myself to go to his funeral.

Throughout these years, I constantly returned to each fragment of information I had secured. I tried to trace George D. Usk, the investigator listed on my Order of Adoption. An Usk was easier to track down than a Cohen or a Fisher, and I soon obtained a phone number in Nassau County. But I was too late: he had died several years earlier.

I returned to Dr. Green, on the pretense that I needed medical attention; I knew that if I told him I wasn't well, he'd have to see me. Perhaps he had softened; perhaps he'd drop some casual hint that would give me another faint track to follow. He reluctantly saw me but his annoyance was apparent from the moment I walked into his office. He had not in the least softened.

Regularly I called St. Anthony's Hospital and returned to 695 Broadway in Williamsburg. *Brush your teeth, comb your hair, and call St. Anthony's.* This became a fixed ritual in my life for years. I was becoming stronger now. I tried different approaches; none succeeded. Either the person I got on the phone would recognize my voice and hang up immediately, or she'd get off, check the files, and then come back and tell me that they were not allowed to give out the information I requested.

Nor did my resolve to comb the area around 695 Broadway produce one shred of evidence that Florence Cohen or Florence Fisher or Frederick Fisher had ever lived there. I went there secretly, never telling my husband; in fact, I told Stan practically nothing, for more than fifteen years of our marriage, about my phone calls to St. Anthony's, my forays to the library, my phone calls to a thousand Cohens and Fishers. Stan is solid and sensible, thoughtful and devoted; I knew he would understand. But from the beginning, I had resolved that this would be *my* search; it was a private affair, and I did not want it to become a burden to someone I loved.

I was beginning to realize the magnitude of the task I had undertaken. It could take ten years. It might take forever. But one thing I now knew with the greatest certainty: nothing would turn up without my effort. I *had* to keep trying.

I knew there was only the slimmest chance, and that each year that chance grew slimmer. I knew I was grasping at straws.

Six

I have discovered that we adoptees have no rights.
                                    —An adoptee

A doctor, a lawyer, a hospital administrator. A thousand
faceless Cohens and Fishers at the other end of phone
connections. Strangers at their front doors; busy shopkeepers. I had confronted individuals and private insti-
tutions who, though they knew, would tell me nothing;
the others I had met or spoken to had nothing to tell.

There was still the court and there was still the law. I
knew now that there were specific regulations governing
the entire practice of adoption; but I had not yet investigated them. When I began my search it never occurred
to me that people would not see that what I wanted was
right and just. I was working in a law firm, and because of
this I began to think there might be some way to acquire
the information I wanted from the court itself.

Would the law somehow provide the first real break?

My work was immensely rewarding. The lawyers were
warm, intelligent, scholarly men, and they took a special

81

interest in me. One of the partners was an established
legal authority, with several published books. While he
was dictating to me, I'd sometimes stop him and ask questions on something he'd said. Once, when he was working
on a paper dealing with the problem of "self-incrimination"
for the *Harvard Law Review,* I had half a dozen small
questions, one after the other.

He looked up with a mock frown and said: "Stop interrupting me. This isn't a classroom!"

But for me it was. I had law books to pore through
during lunch hours and men who usually had time to patiently explain the fine points of law. Several times I was
pleased to hear the partner I worked for say: "That's a
good point, Florence," and then scribble some notes on
his legal pad.

In the mid-fifties, when my papers mysteriously disappeared after my father had visited my apartment, I told
one of the attorneys about the document I had found in
the drawer as a child, that I had secured my adoption
papers but that they'd been lost.

"How did you get those papers in the first place?" he
said.

I told him I had simply gone to the Surrogate's Court.

He was amazed. "Who showed you your file?"

"*What* file?"

"The one on your adoption. It would have contained a
great number of papers connected with your case. But
they're . . ."

"I didn't get my paper from a file." I said I got it from
a large ledger with a heavy binding; it was there with
hundreds of other Orders of Adoption.

"Umm. That should have been sealed, too," he mused.
He looked up at me. "You didn't ask to see the file itself?"

"*What* file?" I asked again.

"Where the rest of your papers are."

I said quickly: "I want it."

He got up from behind his large mahogany desk, came

up to me, and put his arm around my shoulder. "Someone goofed, Florence," he told me. "Your birth certificate should have been sealed or altered, and you should never have been permitted to see your Order of Adoption. All documents pertaining to an adoption are sealed permanently by the state. You'll never be able to get it. Nor, of course, any of the other papers."

"I don't have my paper anymore," I told him, unable to accept his words. "I want it."

He told me that even the ledgers should have been sealed. They probably were within the past few years, under the Domestic Relations Law. It was an oversight, and I had been lucky to gain access to them.

My whole world started to fall away. The attorney went over to his leather-bound statute books, pulled out a large volume, and turned to the Domestic Relations Law that had only recently been passed, sealing all records. First he read a passage pertaining to the Order of Adoption.

"The judge or surrogate shall make an order . . . directing that the adoptive child shall thenceforth be regarded and treated in all respects as the child of the adoptive parents or parent." He looked up to see if I understood this. I nodded. Then he told me that the judge *must* seal the records and withhold them from inspection. "No person," he read, emphasizing certain words, "shall be allowed access to such sealed records and order and *any* index thereof *except* upon an order of a judge or surrogate of the court in which the order was made or of a justice of the Supreme Court." He looked up again, and then continued. "*No* order for disclosure or access and inspection shall be granted except on good cause shown— *good cause,* Florence—and on due notice to the adoptive parents and to such additional persons as the court may direct."

When he had finished this passage, he scanned the next, decided not to read it, and shook his head. "All available information is in those files, Florence—and I'm afraid you'll never be allowed to see them."

I was stunned. I had lost that most precious of documents, and suddenly I knew I might never see it again. Why hadn't I made copies? Worse, why, how had I missed perhaps the one chance I would ever have to secure a *whole file* on myself? They were there—all the papers, even the one I found when I was seven. *Idiot. Why didn' I think to ask? How could I have been so stupid?*

"You've got to help me," I said. "My father can't have taken that paper away from me. It's mine. Isn't there any way to get it back?"

"I'd like to help, Florence," he said. "But those papers have been sealed."

"He stole my papers; he stole my life," I said, beginning to lose control.

I asked every lawyer in the office if he could petition the court for me to open the records. They were sympathetic, all of them, but they thought it was useless. "The Domestic Relations Law is quite clear on that point," one said. "You must show good cause."

"And exactly what is good cause?" I asked.

Nothing, apparently, was good *enough* cause. The matter was left to the discretion of the judge, and none of the attorneys had ever heard of a case in which a petition had ever been made, let alone granted; and they were sure that no sealed records had ever been ordered opened. The records were sealed *permanently*.

I panicked. I had a Flying Dutchman kind of feeling, doomed, because of those records, to wander my whole life and never know the answers I sought.

There was one lawyer on the floor, not attached to the firm, for whom I worked now and then in the evenings. He was a generous, sweet person who never once walked into the office on a night when I was working without giving me a Hershey bar or candy snack. I told him my story and he agreed to help if he possibly could.

Stan and I had little money in those years, and I asked him if I could pay him a few dollars a week for his services. He refused to take any money from me.

"Then I'll do extra work for you," I insisted. "I won't take any pay, and I'll work until you say I've paid off what would be your usual fee."

Reluctantly he agreed; his "fee" ended up being ridiculously low. Some weeks later he told me he had a connection at the court. Then he dictated to me and I typed a letter instructing a clerk in the Surrogate's Court to release that one document, my Order of Adoption. As for the rest, he told me it was absolutely impossible to get the entire file opened.

That same day I took the subway out to Brooklyn. By the time I entered the old building I was a mass of nerves. With the letter, I knew I'd get my Order of Adoption. I also had other plans.

I made the small payment to a clerk of the court for the photostat of my Order of Adoption. The document then had to be secured in another section of the building, but before I took the clerk's receipt, I summoned all my courage and asked in a loud whisper: "Will you take more money and allow me to get photostats of the rest of these files?" This was the first time in my life I had tried to bribe someone.

The clerk's head jerked up. "Absolutely not!" he said. "You have no right to the contents of that file."

"I do," I said quietly, and then, my voice growing stronger with each word: "I'm Anna Fisher—and that's my file. I have every right to see it."

"Impossible," he said. "*You* more than anyone else have no right . . ."

"Who can I see," I said, trying to sound as forceful as possible, "who will allow me *one* look at the contents of my own file?"

"No one."

"There must be someone here at the court who has the authority . . ."

"No. There's no one," he said.

"I want to see a judge," I announced.

He shook his head. "Say, why would you want to look for people who didn't want you, anyway? Don't you owe it to your adoptive family not to go poking around in what's past?"

A perfect stranger—and he was sermonizing me. "I just want the facts," I said. "It has nothing to do with whether my natural parents wanted me or not. It has everything to do with who I am, and what my rights are. I have every right to see those records and that's exactly what I intend . . ."

"You have no right. Those are sealed records. Sealed by the court. Sealed by the State of New York." He shook his head sadly. "Just take this note, lady," he said, scribbling something on a small printed form, "and get your Order of Adoption before we change our minds."

I didn't know whether he had the authority to deny me that order or not; I could not afford to find out.

I asked him where to go, watched as he pointed to the far end of the room, and then headed for my next confrontation. *I'll just get the paper and get out of here,* I thought. *Quick.* I could see there was no chance of getting what I wanted.

The clerk who took the authorization note was quite small, about five-foot-two; he was a dapper little man with patent-leather hair, a small, neat, oiled moustache, and a tight suit jacket on his small frame. He reminded me of an otter or a weasel, or a gloating hotel clerk in a Grade B movie.

He took the paper from me without a word and walked briskly back into a large file room. Everything about the man was brisk, brusque, and officious. In a few moments he came back and placed a large manila envelope on the counter between us.

I looked at it.

He picked it up, took some papers out, and began to finger through them rapidly.

I said to him: "Please, can I see the papers?" I couldn't go without making a try.

He looked up sharply. "Are you kidding, sister?" he said. "This isn't yours. This is a private file, and it's sealed. You're lucky you're getting this much." He had found the Order of Adoption and removed it from the other papers.

"Please," I said softly. And then I heard myself say: "It's my life."

Thinking back on that moment, it is hard to remember more than the emotions. I can remember that people were walking back and forth on the wooden floor behind me, but the room itself is hazy. I remember only the man and me and that manila envelope of papers—and a sense of absolute desperation. I *had* to see them.

"It's my life," I repeated. "Those are my papers. I'm Anna Fisher. *Why* can't you give them to me?"

He looked at the sheaf of papers in his hand, tucked them quickly back into the envelope, and then placed the envelope on the counter again. It was no more than a foot away.

"These records were sealed and they'll stay sealed. You haven't got a chance in a million of ever getting to see these papers. You got to get special permission from the judge, lady, and he'll never give it to you."

"Why?" My eyes were glued to the envelope. I wanted to grab it and run. *It's mine. What can they do to me?* But I couldn't move.

"Well, you need good reason."

I said: "I *want* to see those papers."

"No can do. Just curiosity, idle curiosity, won't open these records," he said, and picked up the envelope. *How dare he tell me that curiosity about myself, about the facts of my birth and my heredity are idle curiosity?*

I watched him take the envelope, along with the Order of Adoption, to a large machine. While waiting for it to warm up, he leafed casually through the papers in the file.

Tears began to fill my eyes. Was it possible that this man could look over my files, could know the facts of my birth—my mother and my father, my origins, everything I hungered for—yet these documents were barred from my sight? Did *he* have a right to this information? I knew he didn't—but he had seen them. Just as any other person in the world, who happened to be born to a legally married couple, and was brought up by them, could come into this Hall of Records and secure *any* papers pertaining to his own life.

Why couldn't I?

I felt so violent I could hardly breathe. When he returned with the copy I'd been authorized to get, he flashed a smile and held the paper out toward me. I was crying profusely and shaking in every part of my body now. I grabbed the paper, turned from him without a word, and bolted out of the building.

The January air did not cool my rage. I leaned against one of the pillars of the building and tried to catch my breath. That envelope, with its faded pencil scribblings, had contained my life. My anger grew. I actually hated *myself* for not taking the envelope and running. Sealed. Those papers were sealed forever now. Once, perhaps, I might have gotten them—when I first went to the Surrogate's Court. But now it was too late, and I was left with only helpless frustration, despair, and rage.

How do they dare pass a law like this? All my doubts and questions began to crystallize as I stood outside the Surrogate's Court, bundling myself in my own arms against the cold winter's evening. *Where were my constitutional rights?*

My mother had carried me in her womb, just like every other child is carried in a mother's womb. My mother conceived me. But these people want me to believe that I was not born but adopted, that my life didn't begin the day my mother gave birth to me—even earlier, much earlier, with my grandparents and their grandparents—but on the day I was adopted.

For a moment I felt as if I was not made of flesh and blood. I felt airy, floating, disembodied. Nothing was firm; I had no roots, only a legally contrived identity.

The lawyers in my office had told me that one of the purposes of the law was to remove the stigma of illegitimacy. How could it pretend to do that when the very sealing perpetuated a stigma? *You're telling me I'm a bastard, and that I have no right to this information. Take what we've given you. Be grateful. Crawl off into a hole and be quiet. Don't come back, because we're not going to help you. You're a bastard, understand? Someone was good enough to take you out of the gutter, and now you're showing that's where you really belong.*

In all the years I'd known definitely that I was adopted, I had never felt soiled; I had felt no stigma. Even when Dr. Green had screamed at me, telling me I had no father, I'd been hurt by his cruelty, his viciousness to me and to my mother, but never ashamed.

I tried to leave the pillar but I could not. I couldn't move my legs. My teeth chattered; my hands were ice cold.

They all talk about what's done for you; they say nothing about what's done to you. You're there to satisfy everyone's needs: your natural mother who, for whatever reason, made her choice and gave you up for adoption; you are supposed to fulfill your adoptive parents' needs to have a child; if there's an agency, they get their cut. And after you've satisfied everybody's needs, all of them decided without your consent, you ask some natural questions. Who was my mother? Whose womb did I grow in? Who gave birth to me? And when you, the innocent issue of an act you did not initiate, want this basic information, they say, "It's idle curiosity, sister. Go away. Be grateful."

I looked back into the Surrogate's Court. Most of the lights were out now. The judges were leaving with their brief cases, the clerks and secretaries were trooping out singly or in groups, laughing or talking.

I am inside that building, I thought. *I am those records and I am sealed, buried alive. The society that withholds those records is telling me that I have no right to myself. Yet he stood there casually holding my file!*

"Idle curiosity?" To know how my mother walks or talks, to see her and speak to her. Why do those secure in the knowledge of who their natural mothers and fathers are tell me I don't have the right to the knowledge they have? How can they presume to tell me how I should think and feel, when they haven't felt and thought the same things—the same ambiguity and longing? The same emptiness.

Why do certain things give me joy and others sorrow?

Why do I feel exalted by beautiful music when I was never exposed to it at home? Why did I save my pennies to go to concerts when I was a child? Why did I paint and sketch and make hats and handbags without any training or the slightest encouragement?

I knew, of course, that there were children who couldn't identify with their natural parents, who found no similarities, no points of contact. It happened. They could see and accept. But when you *didn't* know who your parents were, how could you accept? What lay behind the closed door? *At least let me establish some continuity.*

Blood. Yes, who you look like and walk like are more than idle curiosity. Blood. Whose eyes are behind the great gray void. Blood. How that person smiles or talks or winks or whispers. Those who know have the luxury of saying, "So what?" It's so easy for them. "I look like my father, so what?" When you know, it means nothing; when you don't know, it means your life.

How casually he leafed through my file!

I remember how moved I had been when my son was

born, when I was told, "He looks just like you." Was it all so ridiculous that I wanted to know the two people who had created me, who might look like *me*, who might like music and theater—and life—the way I did?

I am going to beat this thing if it takes until the day I die. Nobody is going to tell me that I have no right to the things they take for granted.

I looked up at the moon. It was now a bright crescent in the cold, dark sky.

I am going to beat the sealed records. I am going to find my mother and father.

Seven

━━━━━━━━━━━━━━━━━━━━━━━━━━━━━━━━━━━━

*Could it really be possible to find the unfindable?
How fantastic it would be to find out something
about my background and heredity!*
                    —A thirty-nine-year-old adoptee

I was overdue for a break. And that first break finally came
—through sheer persistence, refusal to give up, and plain
dumb luck.

But first there was another rebuff awaiting me. I thought
I had faced the cruelest denial of all; but that clerk never
saw me as a person, a wife, or a mother. Mrs. Wax did—
and in many ways her rebuff was the most painful of all.

Every day when I went to work, I passed within a
block of Milton Wax's law office. On a Friday in the late
fifties, I decided to try him again. By now I was older,
stronger, and becoming defiant. I had no reason to believe
Wax would change his position or even see me, but I now
held the conviction that a no is never final: not Dr. Green's
no; not St. Anthony's no; not even the official no of the
sealed records themselves.

There was a new secretary at the receptionist's desk,

and she told me that Mr. Wax had died. I asked to speak with one of his partners. This man was at least willing to see me. "Why is this so important to you?" he asked. "You had a good home, and you've got a good life now—with a husband and a child of your own." He seemed sincerely interested in learning something about a need he had never considered before. So many people had never considered it at all. "Why not let well enough alone?"

I nodded and told him that, yes, my son was nearly grown and gave me much pleasure, and that I had a fine marriage. I had work I liked and a variety of activities I enjoyed.

"Then why do something that might upset everything?" he asked, leaning across his desk. "Why rake up something that's over and done with, that can only cause pain to all concerned?"

Why the assumption always that my search would bring only pain, not happiness and relief, to all concerned?

By now I no longer resented the questions, especially when they came from someone genuinely interested. In fact, I rather welcomed the opportunity to enlighten him. A person shouldn't be expected to live with mysteries, I explained. I felt I had a right to know everything there was to know about myself; I wanted to know—no matter what I found.

"Well, I don't have your records," he said, "and if I did, I really wouldn't show them to you." His voice was pleasant but firm.

"Who has them?" I asked.

He told me that his partner's widow had them all, that by law Mrs. Wax had to hold them for seven years. But he advised strongly that I not attempt to see her, and assured me that she would not let me have the papers I wanted. He refused to tell me where she lived, or what her phone number was.

It did not take me long to get Mrs. Wax's phone number; phone directories were becoming old friends of mine.

The number was still listed in his name. I called, saying only that I wanted to see her on a matter connected with her husband's records. She was reluctant at first, but finally said I could come the next day.

"Your husband was the lawyer for my adoption," I told her when I was seated in her living room. It was a simple room, with well-worn chairs and a sofa covered with a paisley cloth. As I looked around I noticed a set of filing cabinets piled in one corner. *The records.* I knew from my work as a legal secretary that the lawyer would have had to keep duplicates of every paper he filed with the court, including his personal notes on the case. Since the adoption had taken place thirty years earlier, it was possible they'd been destroyed. But they also might still exist; they might well be in one of those cabinets.

I told her my story, and then pointed to the metal filing cabinets.

"I'm not going to keep them much longer," she admitted, but said she had better call her late husband's partner. I looked carefully at her as she dialed. She was about five-foot-three, gray-haired, and very bland. I had the impression she had never, in all the years of her marriage, done a thing without first consulting her husband. I heard her say that I was there. "What do you think I should do?" she asked, looking over to me.

I stared at the filing cabinets, not five feet from where I was sitting, and then back to Mrs. Wax. Not again; I couldn't come this close and fail again.

"Yes," she said into the phone. "Yes, you're right." She hung up and turned back to me. "He says I shouldn't show them to you. I shouldn't get involved."

"It's over thirty years," I told her quietly. "Your husband is dead, my adoptive parents are dead—what interest can you possibly have in whether I look at the files or not?"

"I'm sorry," she said.

"You're a mother," I told her. "The facts of my life are in those papers. They're not important to you, but they're everything to me. Your husband can't be hurt; you can't be hurt. *Please* let me see them."

She smiled and shook her head. "His partner told me not to get involved." She smiled again. Could she possibly be *enjoying* this? Was it possible that she liked the power she had over me? I couldn't believe it. "I don't want to get involved, and I'm sure they're not *that* important to you."

"But the records are *right here*," I said, "in this room. This has nothing to do with your husband's partner. What involvement is there for you? I only want to look at them. Fifteen minutes. That's all I ask, and then I'll never bother you again." What could I say or do to make her show them to me? I turned from her to the cabinets. How could she watch me suffer and not offer to help? I began to cry quietly.

"Didn't you have a good adoptive home?" she asked. *The same questions.* Over and over. From perfect strangers. "That doesn't tell me who my mother and father are."

"You're the child of your adoptive parents," she said. *No, I'm not. And I'm no longer a child.*

To my intense shame, I found myself prolonging the argument, *defending* myself to this woman who now held in her possession papers that were precious to me and meaningless to her. "That doesn't tell me what my natural parents were," I heard myself saying, "or what traits they had that I might have passed on to my own child, that he might some day pass on to his children. Heredity *does* count." And then I was pleading: "Think of your own mother and grandmother, and of your uncles and aunts."

She smiled. "That's an entirely different situation."

"Why is it so different?"

"It's not the same."

"Because you think I was illegitimate?" This wasn't a court. This wasn't society. This was a strange woman, yet here I was baring my soul, as if my life depended upon it. As it did! "I'm not sure I am illegitimate, but even if I am, what difference does that make? Don't I want an attachment to my natural family like other people?"

She had grown annoyed by this time, and asked me to leave.

I threw myself on the mercy of the court. "They're right in that cabinet. I only want to look at the papers. I don't want you to give them to me. I don't want to take anything that's yours."

"I'm sure my husband had his good reasons for not wanting you to see these records," she said curtly. "Once a thing has been legalized, people shouldn't come back and ask so many questions."

"Was *I* a part of that bargain?" I asked, my voice breaking. Maybe *she* could understand. She was a mother, too. "There's a third party to every adoption, Mrs. Wax. What about the child? Don't I have rights?"

"That's really not my affair, is it?"

"It's become your affair." I tried to keep control. I knew that I was annoying her.

"I must ask you to leave right now," she said, her tone firm.

"Won't you *please* let me see them?"

"I don't want to get involved," she said. *Next case!* "I don't want to be bothered by this anymore. You were legally adopted, and that's that. And now I want you out of here immediately."

I felt violent. I wanted to push her aside, yank open the metal cabinets and take my file. I stood up; my legs were shaking. I picked up my coat from the sofa and turned toward the door.

"I don't want you to come back here, do you understand that? I don't want you to bother me ever again," she said as I closed the door.

There was a mountain of resentment building in me; I couldn't believe that somewhere in this world there wasn't one person who would hold out a hand to me.

Every time I went back to these people, I hoped they would change, that they would understand. They never did.

I had called several lawyers about the possibility of petitioning the court to open the sealed records. One said he had spoken to a number of judges, and that they insisted there was not the slightest chance of the sealed records ever being opened. They all tried to dissuade me from pursuing the matter any further, and finally I shelved my plan to petition the court.

Lack of hope did not deter me; it had never deterred me from any other aspects of my search. But in this case, as long as I didn't petition the court, there was always the hope that I *could* petition at some later date, and that they would then say yes. I didn't petition during those years because I knew I could not bear the finality of a no. I knew with certainty that the result would be a no, and I didn't trust my emotions. It was bad enough to be turned down by Mrs. Wax; I simply could not face a judge at that time of my life and hear him say: "You have no right to those records."

With no more concrete leads, no more people to confront, I could only make my morning call to St. Anthony's Hospital, walk aimlessly throughout the Williamsburg area, and haunt the libraries. In the charming Long Island Historical Society in Brooklyn Heights, I found the old Polk's city directories. I was fascinated by them. They were like census books, and contained every man's name, the name of his wife, his occupation, and his address. I spent long and unproductive hours poring over them, looking for Florence Cohen, Florence Fisher, Frederick Fisher—and finding absolutely nothing. I became so desperate for some results, for any results, that I looked up my adoptive name —the names of my father's brothers, some cousins, my mother's sisters. *They* were there—the proper Fisher and Cohen were not. Would all my searching come to nothing more than two pieces of paper?

One day in the mid-1960's, I got up, brushed my teeth,

combed my hair, put on the coffee, and called St. Anthony's. I hadn't called in nearly two weeks; I was slipping.

The voice that answered was one I'd never heard before. The woman sounded quite young. "I'm at Pennsylvania Station," I said breathlessly as I turned the gas up higher under the coffee. "I'm on my way to California and *must* have some information from you immediately."

The young woman asked me what I would like.

"Please go to the files and get the hospital records for Anna Fisher," I said. "I was born at St. Anthony's. My mother's name is Florence Cohen Fisher, and I'm trying to locate my grandparents for my mother." I paused for a second, nibbled at my Danish pastry, and said: "My grandparents have vanished. And I only have a couple of minutes between trains. Please hurry."

"Wait just a minute, please," she said. "I'll get the card for you."

I was still half asleep, and put the phone down for a moment while I puttered around the kitchen, certain she would come back in a moment or so, as had all the others, and say, "I'm sorry, I can't help you" or "We can't give you this information"—or I'd hear the tell-tale *click*.

I heard a faint sound in the receiver and picked it up.

"Now let me see if I have the right papers," she said. I could hear a crackle on the other end of the phone.

I thought fast. "Well, let's compare information," I said, and recited the names and addresses I had first learned from my birth certificate and which had become so much a part of my life. "What else is there? Do you have anything else?" I asked.

The receiver was silent for a moment. *The paper's probably marked. There has to be a statement on it about my adoption. Don't see the statement. Don't see it! Just read off the . . .*

"Well, your grandfather's name was Morris; your grandmother's name was Hannah."

Rapidly: "What was her maiden name? Do you have her maiden name?"

"Sweik. They both came from Russia."

"Anything else?"

She read off the entire card to me. I made her read it twice. Slowly. There was no further information—not an address for my grandparents, no other names.

I hung up the phone in a state of utter shock. I couldn't believe it. But I hadn't written anything down. "Morris Cohen. Hannah Cohen. Hannah Sweik Cohen. Morris Cohen. Hannah Cohen." I kept repeating the names as I rushed around the kitchen looking for a pencil. When I found one and wrote the names down—in bold, forceful letters—I sat looking at the paper. *Could this be it? Could these names be the key? Had someone finally made the goof that would open the locked door?* I could have kissed that hospital attendant.

I had gone back to the lawyer, to the doctor, to the neighborhood; I had made endless phone calls. I had always believed there would be a break.

I turned the phonograph up high. While Giuseppe di Stefano sang Neapolitan songs at the top of his lungs, I danced around the apartment. I danced into the bedroom and looked at myself in the mirror. My eyes were wet and my cheeks hurt from the huge smile of joy that kept widening on my face. *Morris Cohen. Hannah Sweik Cohen. My grandparents.* I looked at myself and, nodding, told my reflection: "Florence, you did it!"

Three months later St. Anthony's Hospital was torn down; all its old records were destroyed.

Eight

Have you ever considered how difficult it is to follow a trail nearly forty years old? People have moved, or died; memories have become faint or feeble; records have been destroyed. Neighborhoods can change character in less time than that. It is hard to go back time after time, alone. It is hard to face the increasing hopelessness of it all, alone. I felt the time approaching when I would have to share my search with someone close to me—my husband, Stan.

Each time I returned to Williamsburg, I could see that it had deteriorated further. The neighborhood I had come to know so well during my periodic visits over more than fifteen years looked even grayer, older now. So did the building on Broadway in which I felt I had my roots, and where I had begun my search. There were still groups of old Hasidic Jews on the streets, with their beards and

inglets, with their black velvet hats, rumpled black frock
oats, black baggy trousers, and black shoes with the
ims of the soles worn away; but the ethnic texture of
my" block was sharply changed.

This time I returned to Williamsburg full of hope. I
ow had four people to search for—my mother, my father,
nd Morris and Hannah Cohen, my grandparents. I
ecognized the possibility that my mother, if she had not
een married, might have lied about her parents' names;
nd, despite my initial elation, I knew that the small store
f information I possessed was old and even unverified.
ut breaking the silence of St. Anthony's had given me
 great boost; if they could make a mistake and let in
 chink of light, I might find light elsewhere as well. Again
 knocked on all the old doors, visited all the old shops,
poke to the oldest members of a local synagogue—always
sking for those four names. No one could give me the
lightest help.

Soon after I learned the names of my grandparents, my
usband suffered some sharp business reversals and I
ad to return to work. For a while I worked for the United
Nations Association, then for a prominent actress on the
roduction of a film, and finally for the New York Phil-
armonic. The job at the Philharmonic paid less than the
thers, but I liked to be near music. During lunch hours I
ould watch the orchestra rehearse, and attend the Friday
natinees; we were regularly given complimentary tickets
nd I often went to evening performances. The job was a
ource of great happiness to me.

For several years, just at the time when I thought the
rucial information had fallen into my hands, I had to con-
ne my search to Saturday odysseys and trips to the main
brary at Forty-second Street. They had micro-film of old
elephone directories, and I would stare intently at the lit
ox in which the endless lists of names were projected.
here were hundreds of Cohens, and dozens of Morris
Cohens in the directories of the late twenties and early

thirties. I knew that Morris sometimes represented a change, in the assimilation process, from Moishe, so I looked for Moishes, too. But I didn't know which of the many names I jotted down could actually be traced more than thirty-five years. It was a hopeless task—and I thought I'd go blind at it.

One morning in early April 1970, as I stood on the subway platform waiting to go to Lincoln Center, I saw an ad for a firm named "Fisher." This had happened many times before over the years, and each time it reminded me that I *still* had not found what I had set out to find. The name always gave me a pang, but this time it triggered a whole series of recollections, and as the subway rocketed downtown, its wheels seemed to repeat that name, *Anna Fisher*.

I thought back to the car accident I'd had a year earlier, and how the nurse at the hospital had asked me whether there was any history of hereditary ailments in my family. Three of my ribs had been broken and it was difficult for me to talk, but I'd managed to tell her that I didn't know. She kept pressing me, telling me I *had* to know, and finally I had told her to leave me alone.

In the succeeding months, as I slowly recuperated, I resolved again to continue my search. I realized I might have died never knowing who my parents were. Stan had insisted I take an extended vacation in Italy, and the slow pace, the music, the joy I'd always felt being with Italians, the long hours lying in the sun, worked miracles and I came back refreshed and strong. The Italians made shrines to the past; ancestry meant everything to them. I had the distinct feeling that I was building my energy for a last stand, that I was going to need every bit of strength I could muster. I wanted *my* ancestry. The need had not diminished; it had intensified.

The name in that ad reminded me I still had not resolved my search. That night, another incident took place. After I had finished working on the details for a new concert

I decided to walk across the plaza to the Met. It was late, but *La Gioconda* was playing, one of my favorite operas, and I thought I might still catch the last act. As I passed through the revolving door, a woman, coming out, took my arm, smiled, and said: "Hello, how are you?"

I had never seen her before in my life.

"Do you know me?" I asked quietly.

"Yes, aren't you . . . ?" And she mentioned a name I'd never heard before.

I shook my head. "No, I'm not," I said. This was always an awkward moment. It had happened many times before, and it was impossible for me to resist. It must sound improbable to someone who has a family, but there was always the chance that I had been mistaken for a relative of mine.

I asked her if we could go to the opera café and have some coffee together. I told her I was adopted and that I'd regret not making absolutely sure she didn't know one of my relatives.

That night I couldn't sleep. The woman had not known a Fisher or Cohen who could be related to me, but the thought that I was still confronting strangers with such questions pained me deeply. I thought of a hundred such confrontations over the years; some of them had been uncomfortable, and I could understand how strange my probing must have seemed to these people. But what could I do? The meager information I'd secured had led nowhere. After nearly twenty years of searching, I was not much closer than I had been on the day Susan first told me I was adopted.

I had searched alone. A few of my closest friends knew I wanted to find my natural parents, and I had still not told Uncle Abe more than the barest facts—that I knew I was adopted and that I had secured my birth certificate. All Stan knew was that once or twice over the years I'd gotten bits of information; I did not want to complicate our marriage.

The next night, as we sat in the kitchen, I realized the time had come to tell him everything. But suddenly I was unable to speak—the tears simply fell.

"What is it, Florence?" Stan said, worried.

I leaned back against the wall and tried to describe the pain, the *physical* pain of not knowing.

"It's my adoption," I told him. "No one has a right to this power over me. What crime have I committed to have been sentenced to a lifetime in limbo? I've made up my mind," I said, "I'm going to find my parents *this year.*"

And then I told him in full detail what I had done over the years.

"I didn't know . . ."

"I've tried to keep it from you," I said. "But I can't bury what I'm feeling anymore. I want to be able to tell you what I've been doing and thinking every day. I need your advice."

He didn't hesitate for a moment. He said: "Let's clean it out of your life once and for all."

◆●◆●◆●◆●◆●◆●◆●◆●◆●◆●◆●◆●◆●◆●◆●◆●◆●◆●●

…t haunts one all through life.

—An adoptee

Every search has a life of its own. Not only do you discover new bits of information, but also something happens to the searcher himself. Slowly, painfully, I had learned a great deal about myself and about the process of searching—how to pace myself, what to say to certain people, and to virtually avoid the word "adopted."

My experience with St. Anthony's had proved how fruitful it could be to go back, time and again, to an original source you knew contained valuable information. Most of the adoptee's records are contained in three or four places—at the hospital at which he was born, in the Surrogate's Court of the county in which the adoption took place, with the lawyer who helped to arrange the adoption, and in the records of the doctor who delivered him.

When these sources, for one reason or another, are sealed off from you, the first tendency after a rebuff is to look elsewhere. But I was changing, and I knew others

might change also. I spoke with more assurance an
analyzed problems with more care. Stan was of particul
help here; his mind was more practical than mine and
the crucial months ahead he helped me reason throug
many of the dilemmas that arose. As I readied myse
for a final decisive push, I decided to return to the ma
I had tried when I first began, Dr. Green.

I had often wondered about Dr. Green's cruelty to m
Soon after our first meeting I saw a play by Robert Ande
son that contained lines so profound that I have nev
forgotten them. "Death is for the living, isn't it? To let u
know it isn't forever, that there isn't enough time to was
on cruelty or meanness or stinginess."

When I couldn't find him listed at his old address, o
at any other address in Brooklyn, Manhattan, or th
Bronx, I called the local medical association and learne
that he had died eight years earlier.

Dr. Green's lawyer, a Mr. Brooks, put me on the tra
of his widow.

Her phone was answered by an answering service, an
by the way she cut in I knew it was her habit to liste
and screen calls before speaking herself. At the soun
of her voice, I decided to tell her I was a foster child an
that I'd been in six or seven homes, from California
New York. I was extremely anxious to know somethi
about my family. Did she have her husband's record.
There might be some note on my mother's card tha
would help me.

Mrs. Green was silent for a moment or two and the
said: "My husband once told me that an adopted chi
had come to him looking for help . . . are you that child'

I knew she knew. Yes, I admitted. I was that *child*—
and asked what he had told her about me.

"That he didn't help you. That he sent you away."

We talked for another ten minutes. She admitted the
were some files and other old things of his around, b
couldn't quite remember where. She said she'd look, an

when I pressed her, said I could call her back in a day or two.

I phoned her the next day and she said curtly: "I looked. I have nothing."

"Are you absolutely sure?" I asked.

"Absolutely," she said. "So there's no point in your contacting me ever again."

Dr. Green's lawyer had been kind and helpful to me on the phone, and I made an appointment to see him. How ironic, I thought, if *Dr. Green's* lawyer became my attorney!

"I lied to you," I said when I was seated in his office. Mr. Brooks was a tall, heavy man in his early fifties. I saw something warm and understanding in his face. "I wasn't a foster child; I was adopted."

"What made you lie to me?" he asked, in genuine puzzlement.

I told him that whenever I said I was adopted, people refused to help me. I paused. "Would you have?"

He thought this over for a moment and then said he wasn't sure.

"That's what this search does to a person," I said.

He leaned across the desk, rested his chin on his folded arms, and said: "How can I help?"

"I want my records. I don't want to be told any more, by anyone, that I don't have a right to them."

He suggested that he petition the court on my behalf. I told him that a dozen other lawyers had investigated this possibility only to throw up their hands. Without a word, he opened his telephone book, jotted down a number, and called an acquaintance of his who was a clerk at the Surrogate's Court. I listened on another extension while he asked about the procedure for preparing a petition. The clerk said that not for any reason would the records be opened. "Why does she want to know?" the clerk asked.

"Well," Mr. Brooks said, "she'd like to know who

her *real* mother and father are. It seems valid to me, and frankly I think she has a right . . ."

"What about the rights of the other people involved?" the clerk snapped. And he ran through the litany: The natural parents have a right to their privacy. They could be blackmailed—*blackmail my own parents?* Natural parents could snatch back their children after they'd given them up. What about the rights of the adoptive parents— and of the children who had been given a secure home?

"This woman is over forty years old," Mr. Brooks said. "Don't you think she has a right to satisfy her curiosity?"

"No," the clerk said. "According to the law she has no right. Don't waste your time."

When he hung up and turned to me he said: "Let me see what else I can do."

"I don't care what it costs," I said extravagantly, "but I want those records—illegally, anyway I can get them. I won't dignify that law by petitioning the court."

"Let me see what I can do first," he said, "before you get yourself into serious trouble."

I told him I wasn't worried about serious trouble.

"I know. You've had a rotten time of it. Let's do this: If I get the information you want, you can pay me $125; if not, the charge will be $50 for my efforts."

This was a ridiculously low figure and I told him so. He said it was fair, and I wrote out a check for $50 as a retainer.

With a lawyer working for me now, and my husband at my side, I felt a sense of growing strength. I virtually took up residence in the New York Public Library and made a discovery. I realized that I hadn't been looking in the books properly; I had spent long hours but my use of Polk's and the old telephone books had been careless, never systematic.

Emboldened by the kindness I had recently encountered, I told the pleasant young man in the genealogy division that I was adopted. He was quiet and thoughtful, as he

xplained that there were many avenues available to me
or tracing the genealogy of my family. He told me that I
hould go back to Polk's. But there was also a virtual
reasure-trove of public information that anyone could
;ain access to, a host of *un*sealed records. Birth records,
leath records, marriage licenses, wills, letters of probate,
·oting registration, census records, immigration records—
.ll these were matters of *public* record and could not be
ealed. I could try The National Archives in Washington,
).C., the Bureau of Vital Statistics, local genealogical
ocieties, the Immigration and Naturalization Service.

They had been there all the time I was looking; I had
imply not realized what was available.

In ten minutes, my whole perspective changed.

I got out that last volume of Polk's, for 1933 and 1934,
nd looked with sharper eyes. Slowly I checked out each
·f the fifty or more Morris and Moishe Cohens in the
3ronx, Queens, Manhattan, Richmond, and Brooklyn di-
·ectories. In each case where the man had a wife, her
ame was listed. Only *one* Morris Cohen had a wife by
he name of Hannah!

When I saw that line a shiver of excitement shot through
ne. I *knew* I was looking at *my* grandmother and grand-
·ather. I was sure I had found them. Then, thinking that
f my mother had *not* been married—as Dr. Green had
nsisted—she would be living with her parents, I went
·ack to those Cohens who had a first name beginning with
he letter *F. Yes.* There was a Florence Cohen living on
Kings Highway, at the same address. I wrote down the
.ddress and then hurried over to the genealogist, showed
.im my birth certificate, my new *find,* and told him about
he information I had received from St. Anthony's.

He looked at me, nodded, and said: "Sure. I'd say that
·ased on what you've shown me, these are your grand-
·arents, and this is where they lived in 1933."

My boss at the Philharmonic, who knew the intensity
vith which I was searching, agreed to let me take longer

lunch hours and I, in turn, promised to stay late when
ever necessary. I was beginning to live in a state of excite
anticipation—like an archeologist or treasure hunter mus
feel when, after a long search, he senses that the end i
in sight.

Two days later I went "home" to the genealogy divisio
during my lunch hour. The same young man with horn
rimmed glasses was there and he greeted me warmly.

He handed me a piece of paper on which was writte
the names of two Florence Cohens. Beside each name wa
a birth date.

"What's this?" I asked.

"Well," he said, in his meditative way, "after you lef
I thought I'd do a little research of my own. I noted you
mother's age at the time you were born, so I checked bac
to the years she might have been born—1909, 1910, an
1911." He looked up from the paper, dropped his glasse
down onto the rim of his nose, and said: "You can writ
for the birth certificates and that may verify your grand
parents' names and even give you other information."

All the years of hostility had conditioned me to in
difference, apathy, and disinterest. "Thank you," I said
moved to tears by his kindness. "Thank you *very* much."

I realized later that sealed records were anathema to
genealogist, whose whole life's work was dependent upo
being able to trace ancestry.

That night I wrote to the Bureau of Vital Statistics an
asked for the birth certificate of Florence Cohen, born
on one of two dates in 1910. I said that the correct cer
tificate would list Morris or Moishe Cohen as her fathe
and Hannah Sweik Cohen as her mother. I signed th
letter "Florence Cohen."

With a new address in hand, my destination for tha
Saturday, April 18, wasn't a bit in doubt. Here was
whole new avenue to explore. *Maybe,* I thought. *Maybe
this time.*

The stretch of Kings Highway at which the Cohen ad

dress was situated had a row of two-family houses, most of them at least fifty years old. Stan and I tried the number listed in Polk's first, but no one living there knew anything about any Cohens. We traced the landlord, but he was senile and remembered nothing.

I then began the familiar odyssey up and down the block; but this was a *new* block, and there was new hope in my heart. We knocked on doors from ten o'clock that morning until nine that night. We spoke to old ladies sitting on stoops, to old men watering their lawns. These were warm, family people, and most of them showed immediate sympathy for a woman looking for her mother. Several of them invited us into their homes, and gave us suggestions about local organizations we might try. One woman had a brother in Florida old enough to have noticed a young, attractive woman my mother's age. I found a public telephone and called him long distance. Incredible as it may seem, he remembered a mother and daughter living on the block. The daughter was sickly, he recalled—and there had been rumors that she had been married and had had a child.

He knew nothing else, and subsequent investigation proved that this was not my family.

About seven, someone told us that the local grocer, a man named Schwartz, had been in the neighborhood for more than fifty years; he might give us a lead.

I had been saying, "I'm looking for my mother" for more than eight hours. I turned to Stan and said, "Please . . I can't say it again."

Stan asked the questions for me, and the grocer, a large and powerful man, became so upset when he heard the story that tears came to his eyes. He thought for a moment and suggested we try a nearby synagogue.

The evening services were over. The rabbi was a man in his mid-fifties—too young, I thought, to have known my mother or grandparents.

His first words were: "Why do you want to find your mother, so you can persecute her?"

I shuddered.

My parents were shadows. I'd never really thought of them as people, rather as the source of answers to the great complex of questions of a lifetime. What did I know of them? They were names on an old birth certificate and an Order of Adoption. They had no reality to me. The last thing I'd ever want to do would be to persecute them. My mother had carried me and given birth to me. I, too, had carried a child and a cord had once connected us, just as a cord had once connected my mother and me. We were all part of each other—my mother, my father, my son, and I.

I looked at the rabbi. He had hurt me deeply and I could not understand why he had said such a thing. Was this what everyone thought? Had this been one of the reasons why the doctor and lawyer had told me nothing?

"Florence?" said my husband.

I held my tongue. I had learned how to control my emotions when I had to, and not fight back. After all, maybe this man could help me. "Why would I want to persecute my mother?" I asked the rabbi quietly.

He had no answer.

He also had no help to give.

Ten

*I don't want to hurt anyone, but is there some way I
can find my natural parents?*

—An adoptee

With the conspicuous exception of Uncle Abe, I questioned
all the members of my adoptive family repeatedly. Soon, I
knew, I'd have to ask Uncle Abe himself—and I dreaded
that moment.

A number of my cousins were adults when I was
adopted, and I was sure they had valuable information.
Uncle Abe, who had lived with us, would probably know
more than anyone else; but I was desperately afraid I
would hurt him by revealing the extent of my longing
for my natural parents.

One evening in mid-May, 1970, I called my cousin Sam.
He told me that he *sort* of remembered some talk about
a family named Zimmerman. He thought this Zimmerman
was the one who had mentioned there was a child available
for adoption.

Here was a new name—unverified, half-remembered,

without a first name: a vague forty-year-old memory that might or might not be accurate, and even then might not prove of value.

Thursday, May 14, I received the call from Mr. Brooks I had been waiting for.

"The records?" I asked.

"No, but I do have information from them."

"I'll be right there."

The information Mr. Brooks obtained—he would never tell me how—cleared up several points. My father, Frederick Fisher, *had* married Florence Cohen in Philadelphia three months before I was born. They separated soon after. Ironically, this was the only information I got from the sealed records; I had amassed far more on my own.

Mr. Brooks had no idea why Dr. Green had told me I was illegitimate. If Frederick Fisher had *not* been my legal as well as natural father, his consent to the adoption would not have been required—my mother could have given me up by herself. The very fact that he *had* signed was incontestable proof that my parents had been married at the time of my birth.

I thought of Dr. Green's insistence on my illegitimacy. Why had he said that? I could have understood if, to protect me, he had said they *were* married if he knew they were not: illegitimacy was still a major stigma then. But to tell me they weren't married, when he must have known they were, was cruel.

Now I had another fact about my life—my parents' marriage—and I felt stronger, and less in limbo, knowing it.

Mr. Brooks said he would write immediately to the Orphans' Court in Philadelphia, requesting a copy of the wedding license of Frederick Fisher and Florence Cohen. I was still waiting for my mother's birth certificate. I didn't know what either of these documents would reveal, but there was always the chance of finding another clue to lead me from the maze.

Saturday, May 16, 1970, was a dismal, grizzly day. It never actually rained, but all day there was a steady fine spray. It was not the kind of day I would have chosen for an extended search. But I wanted to check the Bushwick Avenue address where we'd lived right after I was born, where Zimmerman was supposed to have lived, and then try 695 Broadway for the last time.

Curious images kept flashing in my brain all morning. Three or four blocks from the address, I was able to tell Stan the building would be low, yellow brick, and on the corner. I *knew* the entrance wouldn't be in front but on the side. I remembered being rocked in a wicker carriage by someone in black, and crawling on the floor of a very bright, sunlit room, toward black, high-button shoes.

The building was as I'd envisioned it.

How old had I been when we lived in this house? Only Uncle Abe would know; he was the only person who could tell me about the carriage and the sunlit room and the other mysterious images.

We began to ring doorbells and knock on doors. For an hour we found no one who remembered either my family or the Zimmermans, but then one woman who had been in the building for more than forty years cocked her head and said the name sounded familiar.

Stan and I looked at each other.

Yes, she admitted, she sort of remembered the Zimmermans, or maybe the name was Zimmern, but they definitely had a son—named Hal, or maybe Al—and possibly a daughter. It had been a long time ago and she couldn't remember when they had left or where they'd gone.

These vague recollections were maddening. They tantalized me, holding out all sorts of promise—but you couldn't *touch* them.

Still, it was worth a try and I made a note to check all the Al and Hal Zimmermans and Zimmerns in the four boroughs. With any luck, the telephone directories would only list a dozen or so.

People always wanted to know why you were looking and that meant the same explanations, and then conversations, and then the anticipation while they searched their memories. The more Old World they were, the warmer they were—and the longer the conversations took. I wanted to talk to them; few enough people reached out toward a stranger wandering the streets in search of a mother she'd never seen. The trail was old, and even when they remembered something, their memories were vague and this was even more disturbing for then I had to push them further, and wonder if they *really* knew something. An Italian shoemaker on Bushwick Avenue mentioned that St. Anthony's Hospital had had a special maternity annex in the days when I was born. This was a new lead. I knew the main hospital building had been demolished, and I wondered what I would find—and what I would *not* find.

Somehow the only thing you're really frightened of when you search is that someday there *won't* be an old Italian shoemaker to tell you about a maternity annex he thinks existed forty years earlier, that all of a sudden you'll have seen everyone, every last person there is to see, and have done everything there is to do, and that in spite of yourself and your determination, there will not be another lead to pursue.

We decided to go back to 695 Broadway. As I walked into the building I was forced to admit to myself that it was for the last time; there was no longer hope of a clue here.

But there were still old stores in the neighborhood. One of the clerks, an elderly woman, had once worked in a borough Surrogate's Court. "Adopted people came back to the court in hordes," she said sadly. "Some young, some older than me. And all of them were turned away. I can remember how each of them was asked, 'Why do you want to know?' Many of them weren't sure. Curiosity, maybe. But *I* understood: they wanted to find family."

Yes, family. Continuity. Perhaps that was why. This woman, and many of the women I had met in these old neighborhoods, still lived in a world where the governing philosophy was "family was everything"; they had grown up with it, and they understood. What was new to me, though, was the image of other adoptees looking for their parents. I had thought I was alone. I knew no other adoptees, and one of the most painful aspects of my search was the thought that I alone might be engaged in such a pursuit. I thought how much I'd like to meet other adoptees, to share views and talk about the problems we had in common.

The woman gave me the name and phone number of a man named Kalmus who worked for a local electric company office; he had lived in the area "since the flood" and "knew everyone."

It was after four o'clock now, and we hadn't eaten since breakfast. I wanted to call Kalmus, but first we found a Cuban restaurant and ordered black beans and rice and a small glass of wine. As we sat at the little square table, I realized that, for the first time, I was slowly beginning to get a picture of my mother. She had never really taken form for me before, and I could still not think of her as older than I. She was seventeen or eighteen; I was over forty. I felt like someone watching a play unfold; I was in it, but also outside. She was pregnant—no, not just pregnant: pregnant with me. I didn't have much, but what I had whetted my desire to give her more form—to bring her out of the shadows. I wanted more than ever to see her and talk to her.

When we'd finished eating I told Stan that although this sounded like a far-fetched lead I was going to call Kalmus, and typically he suggested no lead was too far-fetched to follow.

"Tell me, dear," I heard the man say in the phone after I'd introduced myself, "what can I do to help you?"

I said: "I understand you've been in the neighborhood since the . . . for many years."

"Yes," he said. "Many people come to me, and what is it you're looking for?"

I had been saying the words all day. "I'm looking for my mother."

"What do you mean, you're looking for your mother?" His voice sounded concerned, even anxious.

I said: "When I was a baby, I was given away. I'm a grown woman now, with a child of my own, and I'm trying to find my mother."

He became enormously distressed. To this man, whom I didn't know and had never even seen, it was a basic human instinct to look for one's mother. Why *shouldn't* one look for one's mother?

When he got himself together, he began to pour out all sorts of ideas. "Did you look in the telephone directory?" he asked. *How naïve he is and how dear,* I thought. "Tell me, did you go back to the address? Did you go to the hospital where you were born?"

When I told him what had happened at the hospital, he grew furious. "Why?" he shouted at me. "What is the matter with such people? They are monsters, maybe. They got no feelings whatsoever."

"I'm adopted," I admitted, half expecting him to change his attitude.

He snapped back: "So what's the difference? Why shouldn't you look? She's still your mother. A person shouldn't look for her own mother? What's the matter with such people?"

When he asked me if I'd gone to the doctor who'd delivered me, I told him about Dr. Green.

"He threw you out?" he asked, unbelieving. "He should be barred from the practice."

"He's dead," I told him.

"That's good," he said. "I should say this about no man, but Green should be dead."

I told him a bit more about my odyssey, particularly how I had been searching throughout this area. He said: "In any way I can help, will you please let me know immediately? Tell me," and here he lowered his voice, "you need some money?"

"No, no," I said. I was crying and laughing now. *He offered me money. What an incredible human being.*

"You need some money, I want you should promise me you'll come directly to me."

"But you don't know me!"

"That's all right. That's all right. I'll help you. Believe me. You should promise you'll come to me if there is any way in the whole world I can be of any help whatsoever."

When I told Stan, I added: "And he gave me some good leads. There was a Rabbi Risdon who had a congregation in the neighborhood, and he thinks the banks might help. They might have old accounts for one of my grandparents."

When we got outside, Stan said: "You'd better ask Uncle Abe what he knows about your adoption."

I said: "I can't."

"Why not, Florence?" he asked.

"I haven't told him anything other than the fact I know I'm adopted. He still doesn't know I'm looking."

He said he knew I had always rejected the idea because I didn't want to hurt him, but I had to be realistic. Stan said: "He's nearly eighty, and when he goes there will be nobody. Don't wait and then say to yourself, 'Why didn't I do it?' He may be able to provide you with a few clues. He was there. He knew all about the adoption. He may even have seen or met your natural mother. And you know that if he knows anything, he'll tell you."

Stan of course knew Uncle Abe well, for I had kept in close contact with my uncle all through the years. I still had small gifts and mementos he'd given me when I was quite young. In my closet, in a neat cardboard box, I still kept that rose from the birthday cake he'd gotten me the year I had the whooping cough. I knew with absolute certainty that Uncle Abe would not lie to me.

I said: "It will hurt him terribly when he knows I've been searching."

"Florence," said Stan patiently, "he'll understand. He loves you."

Twenty years had passed since I'd learned I was adopted, and now my back was against the wall. Only the week before my son had told me he was going to get married. He had been two and a half when I'd started my search. He was curious when, in his teens, I told him I was adopted—but not upset. The problem troubled him now, too. "Mom," he had said, "don't we have any *blood* relations we can invite to the wedding? Jean's family will all be there."

Stan was right. But, strange as it seems, without those vivid memories as the catalyst, I never could have summoned the courage to question Uncle Abe—not that day, not ever. It gave me an excuse—to track down one specific baffling set of facts—instead of confronting the full implications of asking Uncle Abe about my adoption in general. We found a phone at a corner drugstore and I told Uncle Abe that we were in Brooklyn and that we'd like to take him out to dinner. He said that was a wonderful idea. "Uncle Abe," I said, "there's something I have to ask you. It's terribly important."

"Come on over," he said. "Whatever you want. Whatever I can help you with, it's yours."

Uncle Abe's black hair had long since turned silver-white, and he moved more slowly; but that happy brightness was still in his eyes. We tried to persuade him to go to an elegant restaurant not far away, but it all sounded too elaborate for him. He preferred a local place where he often ate alone or with one of his cronies.

During dinner, I told him we had driven out to Bushwick Avenue, to the building I knew we'd all once lived in. He smiled, remembering. Then I told him of the images I'd had, and how familiar it had all seemed.

"How old was I when we lived there?" I asked.

He thought for a moment and then said: "You were about a year and a half when we moved."

"That's unbelievable!" said Stan.

Uncle Abe told me we had an apartment on the corner and that it was filled with sunlight; he told me how, when my mother had to go upstairs, nuns from the convent across the street would rock me in the wicker carriage he had bought for me. He told me about my grandmother's black high-button shoes, and that I'd often crawl to her and undo her laces. He lowered his head and smiled broadly at me. "She didn't like that."

The time had come to tell him.

I can't do it.

Not with all these people around us.

Perhaps back in his living room, where there were only the three of us, I could say what had been on my mind for so long.

We returned to Uncle Abe's two-and-a-half-room apartment and sat talking about this and that. I could tell he knew something important was on my mind.

Finally my time ran out. This was the most difficult moment I'd had in the entire twenty years of my search. He knew I knew I was adopted, and that I'd gotten my birth certificate. But those things had happened years ago. For some reason, sitting on his couch and looking across at him as he puffed away at a cigarette, I remembered how he used to save Camel wrappers especially for me, and how he'd make little boats and hats out of the silver paper. I'd loved those little piles of silver wrappers; I'd made a hundred designs out of them. He'd always smoked interminably and I smiled as I looked over at him, aging but still healthy, and thought of his story about the doctor who had told him to stop smoking. He'd laughingly said, "If I stop, it'll kill me!"

I leaned toward him finally and said: "Uncle Abe, I have . . . something to tell you . . . and I also have something to ask you."

He nodded.

"I want you to understand," I said, "that what I'm going to tell you has absolutely nothing to do with the way I feel about you. I love you very much. I've always loved you."

He nodded again, but still said nothing.

"In my heart, Uncle Abe, you've always been my father. There's nobody in this world who can ever take your place for me. Not ever."

"What's the matter, honey?" he asked. "What's bothering you so much?"

I said: "It's my adoption."

He said: "What about it?"

"When I found out—you remember, when mother died —I looked a little bit . . . and then . . . and then after that I've never said anything to you about it. I never talked to you about my adoption because I was . . . well, I was afraid that if you knew I wanted to find my real mother and father you'd think it was because I didn't love you."

He smiled slightly and said: "That's foolish. I know you love me. Why would I think that?"

I breathed easier, thinking, *He didn't say, "Why do you want to know?"*

He leaned toward me and said: "What do you want to know? What can I tell you?"

I told him that there were so many traits, so many parts of me that I could find no correspondence for in the Laddens. "I remember how you used to tell me that no one else in the family could dance and sing and sketch the way I could," I said. "How you used to come to all my performances, and how happy I made you."

"You always made me very happy," he said.

"Uncle Abe, there are questions . . . so many questions. I must find my parents, and you're the only person who can give me any answers. If you know anything . . ."

My voice trailed off and I searched his face.

He lit up another cigarette, puffed on it a few times, and then said: "All I remember is that your mother came to me one day and said she wanted to adopt a baby. 'Fine,' I told her. 'Whatever you need, let me know and I'll help you with it.' You see, I felt I was getting a baby, too. But after that it became a vague, silent thing in the house. She never told me any of the details. I seem to remember that something was said about your parents coming from Philadelphia, and that it had been an early marriage that didn't work out. It's terrible but that's all I know. I wish to God I could tell you more."

I leaned over and kissed him on the cheek. I knew that if he could have taken me by the hand and brought me directly to my mother and father he would have done so. My foolish fears had never materialized, and I was desperately sorry I hadn't come to him years earlier. Admittedly, there was nothing new in what he told me— but I left his apartment that night feeling good and clean inside. I knew that this source was exhausted, and that not for one moment had I gotten the impression that he thought I didn't love him.

Now I had another person, a person close to my heart, with whom I could discuss the problem at any time. *How stupid I've been,* I thought, *to forget that where real love exists there can be no resentment—and there should be no guilt.*

Eleven

I raise Irish setters, and it's a little disturbing to know that I can trace their pedigree further than I can trace my own.

—An adoptee

They were terrible letdowns at the time, but it is amusing to think back now on some of the red herrings, the wild-goose chases I followed, some of the foolproof systems that—until the last moment—fooled me.

I reasoned that all I had to do was go back to the 1932 telephone directory, the year the last edition of Polk's was compiled, and find the Morris Cohen listed at the Kings Highway address; then I would check each of the subsequent telephone directories until this Morris Cohen disappeared or moved to another address. With any luck, I'd be able to find a much more recent address, quite possibly one where the family had lived for long enough to establish close relationships with the neighbors. One of these neighbors might then be able to tell me at once where my grandparents were or, if they were dead—which was a distinct possibility—where I could find my mother. I told

Stan and he thought the theory was sound. I couldn't wait
to test it.

In the microfilm room of the New York Public Library,
I ordered the film for the summer 1932 Brooklyn telephone directory. In those days, the directories came out
several times a year, and I had randomly chosen this edition with which to begin. Yes, there *was* a Morris Cohen
at the Kings Highway address in the summer of 1932. I
am by nature neither mathematical nor scientific, and the
thought that I had finally developed a system to beat the
black past thrilled me. *Now,* I thought, *all I have to do is
trace the Cohens through ten or fifteen years, figure out
where they moved, and I'll be that much closer.* This was
going to be easier than I thought!

I immediately took out the film for the winter 1932
directory. Rapidly I spun the knob until I came to the
Cohens.

My Morris Cohen was not there!

I went back over the list, looking at each address carefully. *He couldn't appear only once and then disappear.
Couldn't he have stayed at Kings Highway for at least
one full year?*

On a pad I wrote down the names of all the Morris
Cohens who appeared in both directories—the summer
1932 and the winter 1932. By carefully collating the two
lists I discovered that there were three Morris Cohens
in the summer directory who did not appear in the winter
edition. There were also three *new* Morris Cohens in the
winter edition who had not appeared in the summer edition.

Of the three new listings in the winter telephone directory, one lived on Myrtle Avenue (and had two addresses,
one his office as an attorney); the other lived on East
Nineteenth Street; and the last Morris Cohen had an address on Avenue J. This suggested several possibilities.
None of these names could be his. Or he could have
moved to one of the new listings in Brooklyn. I was

certain he had not been a lawyer, so I eliminated this name. That left only two Morris Cohens.

As I went home that night, I laughed to myself as I thought of how he had appeared only once, like a phantom. There was something deliciously humorous in the abrupt collapse of my theory. But that night I promptly came up with a brilliant new theory.

The next day I hurried to the library, going first to the winter 1932 telephone directory in the microfilm room and then to the Polk's city directory in the genealogy division. I checked each Morris Cohen in Polk's against each one in the telephone directory. Beside the telephone listings I filled in the names of the wives. By this method of double-checking I was able to account for every Morris Cohen listed in both directories. Clearly, if Morris Cohen of Kings Highway had remained in Brooklyn, but moved to another address, he now either lived on East Nineteenth Street or on Avenue J.

Morris Cohen on East Nineteenth Street in the winter telephone directory had moved there from Third Avenue —the wife's name in both cases was the same; this now eliminated him as a possibility at the Avenue J address. Thus Morris Cohen newly located at Avenue J moved there either from Kings Highway *or* from somewhere else. I checked telephone directories and Polk's for every other borough and found no Morris Cohen with a wife named Hannah.

Morris Cohen on Avenue J *had* to be my grandfather. Everything pointed to this deduction. So I got out the film for every Brooklyn telephone directory from 1933 through 1970.

Morris Cohen finally vanished from Avenue J in 1963— thirty years after he had moved to that address. The trail might still be warm. I had every reason to believe that there would be people living at the Avenue J address who would remember a man who had positively lived there for thirty years, and who had only left seven years ago

I decided to play another hunch and check the city directory for a Zimmerman. I wanted very much to place the Laddens and the Zimmermans, or the Cohens and the Zimmermans in one place at one time. If Zimmerman had served as a go-between in the adoption, he might well have known both families intimately.

In the 1933 Polk's city directory I found a Louis Zimmerman listed at the same address at which my Morris Cohen lived!

Even better, this Louis Zimmerman was an attorney, with an office in Brooklyn. I quickly theorized that Cohen and Zimmerman were contemporaries, and Zimmerman might well have arranged the adoption for the Cohens. Wax had been the attorney for the Laddens, but this Zimmerman might have known Dr. Green, the Cohens, and the Laddens, too. He might be the central figure in the drama.

It was too coincidental—Zimmerman and Cohen in the same building. What had probably happened was that Zimmerman had learned that his friend's daughter was pregnant and, as an attorney, had made the contacts that finally led to my adoption. I had asked Uncle Abe about the name "Zimmerman"; he said it sounded familiar. The more I thought about what I'd learned, the more certain was my re-creation of the situation was correct.

Several hours later, I learned that Zimmerman dropped out of the book in 1964; I phoned his law firm, which I had traced to Manhattan, and found he had died seven years earlier; I tracked down his widow to a new address.

I called Mrs. Zimmerman at once and asked if she had lived at the Avenue J address and if she knew a Morris Cohen.

She said she had lived in the building for twenty-three years but that she couldn't remember anyone by that name.

Mrs. Zimmerman mentioned that her husband's friend Dr. *Fred Fisher* had died some years earlier, and that she knew the name Ladden; one of my adoptive cousins, it turned out, was her closest friend. Later, Stan said that everything was too suspicious to be coincidental. Zimmerman, Ladden, Fisher. Why would she have lied about not knowing a Morris Cohen? People had lied to me before, but I felt instinctively that Mrs. Zimmerman was *not* lying; she had been too straight-forward with me throughout the conversation.

There was only one definite way of checking out the whole story—go to Avenue J. I was planning, of course, to do that anyway. The decisive name would be that of Morris Cohen's wife. His name was common, but there could be no doubt if this Morris Cohen had a wife named Hannah and a daughter Florence.

On Saturday I drove out to Avenue J to ring doorbells. It took only an hour to find a man who knew Morris Cohen. Yes, he said, Morris Cohen had definitely moved in 1964, the year Morris disappeared from the phone book. I pressed further. Did he know where the man was living now? Did he have a daughter?

Yes, they were friends and had kept in close contact after the separation.

"Morris Cohen," he said, "is now living in Tucson, Arizona, with his only child Albert and his wife Bella."

When you search, something comes of everything.

The only salvageable bit of information from the entire sequence of events was the phone number Mrs. Zimmerman gave me of my adoptive cousin. I could have gotten this elsewhere, but I doubt I would have thought of calling her. I hadn't seen her since I was a child, and wasn't sure she'd remember me.

My cousin confirmed a fear I'd submerged since I first saw my birth certificate. My adoptive parents had been highly orthodox, and would therefore have regarded it as a sin to name a child after a living relative. My mother had told me I was named for my dead paternal grandmother, whose name had been Florence. Until that moment, I had assumed it was an accident that my natural mother's name was also Florence. My cousin assured me positively that my paternal grandmother had been named *Sarah*.

My adoptive mother had known the names of my real father and mother. She must have deliberately named me Florence. Along with the developing picture of my natural mother, I was, over the years, learning more and more about my adoptive mother. I realized fully now how desperately possessive she had been, how little she could control her obsessive acts. She must have thought once she named me Florence my natural mother *was* dead and could never return to claim me.

On Friday evening, when I returned from work, an envelope from the Bureau of Vital Statistics was waiting for me. Inside was my mother's birth certificate. This gave her still more substance. The only minor discrepancy concerned my grandfather's first name; it was listed as Moishe instead of Morris, but I'd long realized that this assimilation change might have occurred. My grandmother's maiden name was again listed as Sweik.

My mother's place of birth was shown as 80 Morris Avenue; she had obviously been born at home. Although Stan said an address sixty years old was really scraping the bottom of the barrel, on Saturday May 30 we drove to Morris Avenue. The area was in a state of total collapse. The streets were littered with garbage; there were sooty factories with their windows planked over; and the dreary wood frame and dirty red-brick two and three-family houses had broken or boarded-up windows and torn shades or half curtains. I tried to see it as the clean, neat post-Victorian sector it had once been. Perhaps my mother had played on these streets.

We drove slowly down the block and checked carefully for numbers. Seventy-four, seventy-six, seventy-eight—and then eighty-two. Between seventy-eight and eighty-two there was nothing but a huge hole! I stared at the excavation that had once been 80 Morris Avenue and burst out laughing. This time I had really gone back to my roots.

The first week in June was extremely busy for me. The Promenade concerts were in full swing, and several nights I stayed on after my work. I had begun to collect my notes, and to make a detailed diary of all that had taken place, a full record of my investigations. Each day I added more details or thoughts. I kept trying, as I looked at the names and places and dates, to find new clues.

I kept the door open while I worked, so I could listen to the concerts. The music was soothing and enabled me to think more clearly. What hadn't I done? I hadn't yet checked the Kings Highway area for voting registration. What about schools my mother may have attended? Were criminal records worth checking? Would anything be gained by writing to the Bureau of Motor Vehicles for driver registration or license information? Death certificates? At least one of my grandparents might have died. Will probates? Everything hinged on whether they had continued to live in Brooklyn after 1933; if they had moved out of the city, or out of the state, then *all* my searching through New York records would have been a waste.

By the end of that week I felt exhausted. On Thursday night, I had great trouble falling asleep, and when I did I dreamed I had found my mother. In the dream I came to an old brick building, two stories high, and climbed the loose wooden stairs to the second floor. I couldn't believe that I'd actually found her. The anticipation of our meeting was almost more than I could bear. The door opened at my knock, and a smallish woman, dressed in black, appeared. She looked sad and tired, and when I said, as I had so many times before, "I'm looking for my mother," she answered in a quiet monotone: "Your mother died yesterday. You're one day too late."

I closed my eyes and held on to the frame of the door. "You've got to bring her back to me. I've got to talk to her. I'm Florence."

The woman said, in the same monotone: "She died yesterday. There's nothing I can do."

"No, not yesterday . . . not after all . . ."

In the morning the alarm was only a dull sound in the back of my brain, and the echo of it, perhaps, was what woke me. I was late for work and rushed out of the apartment, disturbed by the memory of my dream. *She's not dead. There's a chance that she's dead, but she's not. I know she's not.* I wanted to find my mother *that* day, before it was too late.

When Mr. Brooks called and said he'd received my parents' marriage certificate from the Orphans' Court in Philadelphia, I threw on my coat and ran out of the office.

My hands trembled as I took the certificate from him: this was the first time I'd seen my parents' signatures.

The names and dates leaped off the page. February 28 was the date of the marriage. I had been born in May of that year. Again I had a visual image of my mother. I saw a small dark-haired girl—as I had been—with the short bobbed hair of the prohibition years. She was very young, very pregnant, and very desperate. My heart broke for her. She had lied about her birthday: on the license she was twenty-one but I remembered that the date on her birth certificate would make her only seventeen. Her mother's name was given as Hannah Sweik Cohen.

I sat down in Child's Restaurant for a long overdue breakfast. I stared at my mother and father's wedding license. *I have a real mother and father!* The sealed records had made an orphan of me; but now I was no longer an orphan.

My father's occupation was listed as clerk, and his place of residence Philadelphia. I still couldn't quite put Philadelphia and New York together. Was it possible that there were *two* Cohen families involved, and that the one I had been tracing in New York was no relation to me?

There were street addresses for both my parents, and I decided to go to Philadelphia the next day, a Saturday, to check these out.

I was unable to control my joy. It was not that I now knew my parents were definitely married or that, technically, I was legitimate—but that they *were*—that they existed. Their handwriting gave them a greater reality than I'd ever felt before. This was the first concrete touch of them I'd had. Their signatures gave them life.

The marriage certificate also gave my paternal grandparents' names—Jacob and Irene—and my grandfather's occupation, designer. It did not say what he designed, but I assumed it had to be clothes. Although I had never studied designing, it had always come naturally to me.

That night I got out all the documents I had acquired—my birth certificate, my Order of Adoption, my mother's birth certificate, and the wedding license. The one name that tied all the common names of Cohen and Fisher together, that assured me that all these papers referred to one family, my family, was that of my maternal grandmother—Hannah *Sweik* Cohen.

As we drove to Philadelphia, I began to wonder, for the first time, whether I had any brothers or sisters. I hadn't thought of such things before, but now that my parents were beginning to take form in my mind, I began to think of whether they had new families.

Mostly I thought of my father; the marriage certificate had been my first concrete evidence of him. I was going to Philadelphia that day to look for *him*.

We drove to Walnut Street, to my mother's address as listed on the marriage certificate. We asked everyone about Fishers and Cohens, but no one in the neighborhood remembered my mother, my father, or any of my grandparents. We found a local synagogue. Nothing. At the Chestnut Street address where my father had lived, we thought the break had come. The woman who answered the door was the owner; she said she had owned, and lived in, the building for forty-four years.

"Forty-four years?" asked Stan.

"That's right."

Eagerly I asked her about Frederick and Florence Cohen Fisher, saying they had lived in one of her apartments during the late winter of 1928.

She said she had a perfect memory for such things; they definitely had *not* lived there, neither of them, singly or together, at any time.

Phantom Cohens and phantom Fishers.

And another wild-goose chase.

Twelve

On June 26, 1970, I saw my mother for the first time. All the pain I had felt at the censure and even the contempt of those determined to wall off my identity fell away. No more need I ever hear the objections, "Why do you want to know?" "You have no right to know." No more would I have to lie or search through the labyrinths of dead records. The longing ended. I knew why I had searched and what I had searched for, and my life was changed forever.

Now, as I think back on the three weeks that preceded that event, they seem to press inescapably toward the day I first saw her—I so tense and she so unsuspecting. But while those weeks passed, I knew only that I had to summon my greatest will and ingenuity, that something lay beyond the old directories and dead documents. I did not know until the last moments how close I was.

The old telephone directories in the library annex on Forty-third Street and Eleventh Avenue are yellowed and falling apart. Many of them have no bindings and are tied together with string. The leaves are loose, and some are so dry that the cheap, thin paper comes apart in your hands. On Monday, June 8, during my lunch hour, I searched but found no Fishers on Chestnut Street in the 1928 Philadelphia telephone book. I did find a Morris Cohen at the Walnut Street address.

I now *knew* that these people had once actually existed —though there seemed a positive conspiracy afoot to keep me from finding them—but each time one of those names appeared among the thousands of faceless names on a microfilm projector or a yellowed telephone book page, I felt a little surer.

There were times when I needed that assurance.

The Morris Cohen on Walnut Street positively confirmed that my mother had lived, for at least a short time, in Philadelphia; she must have returned to New York at the time of my birth.

A new idea began to form in my mind. I had already reasoned that one or both of my grandparents had died. If they had died within one of the boroughs of New York City, there would be a death certificate on file. Such certificates would list the place of death, the name of the informant, the funeral chapel that handled the last rites, and the place of burial. There were summary books in the New York Public Library, issued yearly; these contained alphabetical listings of all persons who had died in that year, the date of death, the borough in which death occurred, the certificate number, and age at time of death.

Why hadn't I thought of this before?

Had the thought of going through death certificates frightened me?

On Friday night, Stan drew up a series of charts for my maternal grandparents. The age of each had been listed on my mother's birth certificate—but without month, day, or year of birth. Stan charted their approximate ages at any given year, based on their chronological ages at the time of my mother's birth. For each year, from 1933 to 1970, there were three possible ages my grandparents might be. In 1963, for example, my grandfather would have been eighty, eighty-one, or eighty-two. This chart would enable me to tell at a glance whether a particular Morris or Moishe Cohen or Hannah Sweik Cohen could be one of my grandparents. He also drew up charts for each of my parents.

Early on Saturday, June 13, I went to the New York Public Library. I dreaded the thought of checking through the death summary books.

Since it was more likely that they had died—if, indeed, they were dead—in a recent year, I decided to check back from the latest date to 1933, the last date I knew they were definitely alive. The books for 1968 and 1969 were not yet available, so I began with 1967, checking for Florence Cohen, Frederick Fisher, Florence Fisher, Morris Cohen, Moishe Cohen, and Hannah Sweik Cohen. Each time I found one of those names I checked the age of death against the chart my husband had prepared for me.

As I progressed, year by year, through the death summary books, jotting down the possibilities that appeared, I realized that this, of all the hopes I'd had over all my years of searching, was the best: the certificate would list next of kin. One or both of my maternal grandparents *had* to be dead; otherwise they would be close to ninety. It was a terribly humid June day. As I worked, bending over the ledger books, straining to see each name, I began to grow dizzy; it seemed as if the room was growing darker and darker.

No. There was a deeper reason.

All my life I had wanted grandparents. All I'd ever known was my adoptive grandmother, with her old heavy-knit maroon sweater and high-button black shoes, sitting in our living room all those years, poking me when I came near, calling me *"momser."* I had tried to like her. I remembered sitting on the old grandfather's lap in the home of the Italian family in Brooklyn. I remembered how much I'd wished that he was *my* grandfather—with his songs and warm eyes—or that I had a grandfather like him.

Now I was sitting in a hot little library room hoping desperately that one of these names of a dead person was my real grandmother or grandfather. Each time I wrote down a name and age at death and checked it against my carefully prepared chart, I was hoping that one of my grandparents was dead. Only if they were dead could I hope to find, through next of kin or informant, my natural parents.

I found a Hannah Cohen, age seventy-nine, who had died in 1967. The possible ages on my chart were seventy-nine, eighty, and eighty-one.

There was a Moishe who had died in 1961, aged seventy-nine. My chart listed seventy-eight, seventy-nine, and eighty.

Another Moishe had died in 1957, at seventy-five. My grandfather could have been seventy-four, seventy-five, or seventy-six in that year.

These were all in Brooklyn. In the other boroughs I found twelve others, and listed all the pertinent information about each of them. There was a Florence Cohen, who had died in 1948 at the age of thirty-six; my mother would have been thirty-seven or thirty-eight that year. The age was not exact. I dreaded to think my nightmare had been prophetic and that my mother was dead—but I listed the name anyway.

As the hours wore on, searching death records became more painful to me than knocking on the doors of a thousand strangers. I thought: *This can't be me, praying that one of my own grandparents is dead*. Perhaps I had not intensified my search earlier, I realized, because I was *afraid* of just such a trauma as this. Finally I could no longer bear the strain. Without saying good-bye to the

librarians, with whom I'd grown so close over the past
months, I clutched up the lists I'd made and rushed from
the room.

On Wednesday, June 24, I made myself up carefully; if
the clerk was a man, it might give me an edge to look my
best. My destination was the Bureau of Vital Statistics to
ask for the death certificates of the three Cohens who had
died in Brooklyn. This would eliminate, I hoped, the four-
to five-week wait incurred by going through regular channels.

I had a strong feeling that something was about to break.

Over the years I had learned not to be tentative with
those in authority—not to say "may I," but "I would like
to" see. I told the first clerk I saw that I'd like to have
copies of the three death certificates.

He said: "Sorry, you'll have to write for them."

"I'm only in town for a few days," I said, "and I *must*
have them now."

He said it was against regulations.

I walked directly to the desk of another clerk.

I pleaded with him for ten minutes.

He said: "You'll have to make the proper application."

The make-up I'd put on so carefully began to run. I
took out a handkerchief and put it to my eyes.

He looked at me for a moment. I made no move to
leave. Then he smiled, threw up his hands, and said: "All
right. All right. You'd get them anyway. I'm not going to
stand in your way. Let's have a look at your names."

He took the paper, with its three names and death dates,
and asked another clerk to get him the books for 1967,
1961, and 1957.

The ledger book for 1961, containing all the original
death certificates for that year, came up first. While we
sat waiting for it, I'd told the clerk of my twenty-year
search, never mentioning that I was adopted.

By the time the 1961 ledger book came up, he was so
interested in my hunt that he took the book himself and

physically turned the pages for me, while I looked on. I could see that he was getting more and more excited. In a few moments he came to Cohens whose first names began with M.

"Aaaah," he said, his finger sweeping down the page and stopping at one of the names. "See, see. Moishe Cohen. Here it is!"

And there it was.

I read the date of death, the address of the deceased, the cemetery, the date of burial, the funeral home, the place of death, and then the name of the informant: *Hannah Cohen*.

"See," the clerk said excitedly. "It's Hannah. That's right, isn't it? Hannah."

"Yes," I said quietly. "That must be my grandfather." That paper had more reality than any family I had ever known.

When the next ledgers came up together a few moments later, I told him that since we'd found a Moishe with a Hannah as informant, we should check the 1967 book first, for the death of Hannah Cohen. Again the clerk ruffled through the pages; he seemed almost more anxious than I to find the certificate. In a few moments he came to the Cohens, and then I heard him cry: *"Yes!"*

There it was, for the second time in ten minutes.

The address of deceased was different, but only several houses away on the same block. She could have moved. The same funeral home was listed, and they were buried in the same plot, in the same cemetery. The name of an old-age home in which she had died was also given. Then I saw the clincher: the maiden name of the decedent was *Zweick*.

Before I could say a word, the clerk said: "This is it! Zweick. Sweik. Zweick is the Russian. You've found it!" There was a tremendous smile on his face, and he patted me on the arm.

I could only nod. I was too filled with mixed emotions

to answer. There could be no question this time. No red
herring. This had to be them. These were *my* grand
parents.

As I looked down the page there was a new name, an
it puzzled me. The next of kin was listed as Norman Cone
This was followed by the word "son," and then an address
My mother's birth certificate had listed her as the onl
living child of my grandparents; however, through a chec
of other directories I had been able to determine that sh
had a younger sister. I knew nothing of a brother. Was i
possible that I'd made a mistake again? Could this be
different family? No, not necessarily. This might be
younger brother, my uncle. He might have changed hi
name. "Cone" was a logical change from "Cohen." Bu
did that mean he was the only survivor? What had hap
pened to my mother? And her sister?

I felt tense and overexcited and although it was a ho
day, I wanted to walk it off. Mr. Brooks's office was nearby
I wanted to tell him. I could sit there, sip a glass of col
water, and collect my thoughts.

It was four thirty when I finally arrived at the office.
put both photostats on his desk and slumped back int
one of his huge leather chairs.

"These *have* to be your grandparents," he said excitedly
"If they aren't, your mother had a twin sister who di
everything she did, lived every place she did. Sweik
Zweick. There's no doubt about it. Your grandmother'
maiden name . . ." I nodded. He asked: "What are you
going to do now?"

I said: "I'm going to the funeral home."

"Why don't you wait until tomorrow, Florence? You
look worn." He examined the photostats for a moment and
then realized a close friend of his was a director of the
old-age home mentioned on my grandmother's death cer
tificate. He phoned his friend, who authorized him to cal
the main office and to use his name. Mr. Brooks did so,
asked for someone in charge of the records, and pleasantly

requested the next of kin for Hannah Zweick or Sweik Cohen. He held the phone away from his ear and I heard a woman's voice say that they couldn't give out such information on the phone. Mr. Brooks said he had the authority of the director, and that they could call him if they had any doubts.

As I heard Mr. Brooks pressuring the woman gently, I kept thinking of all I'd been through. Dr. Green, Milton Wax, the nun at St. Anthony's, the clerk in the Surrogate's Court, the Rabbi, the countless hours on the streets and in the library, the endless questioning and ambiguity and searching.

"Yes? Yes?" he said, looking over to me. "Florence . . . Okun? *Florence?*"

I gasped.

"And you can't give me anything else?" he asked. "Not an address? Not the names of the other children?" He looked over at me and shook his head. "All right," he said into the phone. "Yes, thanks very much."

He turned to me and said: "Florence Okun."

"Yes," I said softly.

"We'll get the rest tomorrow, Florence," he said, looking at his watch. "I've really got to catch a train."

But I had searched too long, too hard, to wait. Certainly another day would not mean much to most people; but I had dreamed of being one day late—and finding my mother dead. No, I would not wait another day. I wanted the information that night—all of it: names, addresses, phone numbers.

When Mr. Brooks left, I dialed the home myself, told the woman I was Mr. Brooks secretary and that we needed information about the Cohens urgently. She protested, but I pressed her.

The phone was silent for a moment. Then I heard: "Exactly what information do you need?"

She gave me the name of my mother, Hannah Zweick Cohen's daughter—and her address, her home phone number, and her business phone number. She gave me the name of my uncle, Norman Cone, and his address and phone number.

Now it was all confirmed. There could be no doubt whatsoever. These were *my* grandparents, who had lived on Kings Highway in 1933; this was *my* uncle, no doubt the youngest, and perhaps not listed in Polk's, which didn't list minors. This, Florence Okun, was *my* mother—and I had her current address and phone number.

I did not hesitate a minute. I dialed the number of Florence Okun.

"Is Mrs. Okun there?" I asked.

The woman said: "No, there's no Mrs. Okun at this number."

I looked at the pad on which I'd written all the names, addresses, and phone numbers. Digit by digit I gave the woman the number I wanted. Yes, it was correct. But she had had that number for about a year and did not know who had it before that.

No matter, I thought as I hung up. She might have changed her number. *I've found her.*

I scribbled all the information I'd gotten on Mr. Brooks's desk pad, and left it propped against his telephone.

In the elevator I noticed that people were staring at me; I may have been talking to myself. *I've found her.* Waves of relief, exaltation, and disbelief flooded through me. It was not another dead end. I *had* found her.

Stan and I sat in the Italian restaurant until well after midnight. I ate pasta and scampi, and a large antipasto. I drank four glasses of Valpolicella. The waiter, a pudgy little Italian, asked me why we were celebrating. When I told him I'd found my mother, he said: "Where did you loo-sa her?"

Then I said to Stan: "I've got to go out there tonight."

He had lived these last months with tremendous closeness to the search, and it never occurred to him to ask: "Why don't we wait until tomorrow?"

She was real now: she lived in an actual house. Dobbs Ferry wasn't Brigadoon; it wouldn't vanish. I wouldn't disturb her. I really had a mother; and I wanted to see something tangible—the house my mother lived in.

It was two o'clock by the time we found the dimly lit street in Dobbs Ferry. Tree-shaded and lined with simple but comfortable one-family houses, it looked like it would have been pleasant to grow up in such a neighborhood. We followed the numbers until we finally came to 127. There were no lights on. Stan stopped the car and I leaned far out to see the name on the mailbox. I couldn't make it out and asked him to back the car up a few feet and put on his brights. He did so.

The name on the mailbox was F. X. McDowell.

"Wait," Stan said. "I'll ask those kids." There were teen-agers necking in a parked car directly across the street. He got out of the car and walked slowly over to them. I watched him tap on the window, saw two heads suddenly jerk up, and then the window roll down.

Stan walked back slowly. Something was troubling him. He looked at me for a moment with trepidation, as if to say, "Should I or shouldn't I tell her?" I didn't say a word. Then, cautiously, he said: "I asked them if the Okuns lived there."

"What did they say?"

"They moved away a year ago."

"Oh, no!" I shouted, and began to laugh uncontrollably.

"Florence, are you all right?"

"All right? Of course I'm all right." This was not a case of the phantom Cohens again. This time there was no mistake. They had lived here and now they lived someplace else. "Where can she go in one year," I said, "that I can't find her? Where in the world can my mother go that I can't find her now?"

3

Somebody's Child

Thirteen

I feel a tremendous need to see and talk to my real mother, if only once and for one minute. With all my heart I hope to find her someday, before it's too late.
                                                    —An adoptee

I dialed the number quickly and asked: "May I speak to Mrs. Okun please?"

We had not arrived home until nearly four in the morning, and I could hardly sleep. Although physically and emotionally exhausted, my mind spun with expectations. The first thing I did when I got to the office the next morning was to check the Westchester telephone directories for 1967, 1968, 1969, and 1970. There was a William B. Okun listed; and at the same address a Marsha Okun. There was a Robert L. Okun at another address. They were in all three books but not in the current directory. I still had my mother's office phone number; though they'd moved, she might still be working there. If it was a small firm or if she had a private phone, perhaps it was she who would answer.

"I'm sorry," a woman told me. "Mrs. Okun doesn't wor
here anymore."

I said: "Can you tell me where she *does* work?"

"No," the woman said hesitantly. "Who is this spea
ing?"

"I'm just in from California for a couple of days,"
said, "and I'm not sure I have the right people, but I'
trying to trace my grandmother's family. I believe M
Okun is a cousin of mine, and I'm terribly distressed b
cause I just found out she moved from Dobbs Ferry
year ago. Can you possibly tell me where she moved?"

"Oh, is that all?" the woman said. "Mrs. Okun move
to Manhattan last year."

I asked: "Does she have a daughter named Marsha
"Why, yes."

I now knew, for the first time, that I had a sister.

"And a son named Robert?"

"Yes, she does."

"Does she have any other children?" I asked.

"No. No more children that I know of."

When I hung up, I got out the current Manhattan dire
tory. Okun was a great name. Smith, Jones, or Cohe
would have finished me! My mother and her family we
all listed. She had done exactly what I'd do. She had raise
her children in the suburbs and then retired to Manhatta
—perhaps to be near the theater and opera. She had re
tired to *live,* not to die. I knew her. I also, inexplicabl
had an overwhelming sense of protectiveness toward he
To me, she was still, somehow, seventeen years old; I sti
felt like *her* mother and I thought, *I must protect her;
must be very careful, very tender.*

I dialed her home number. The phone rang once, twic
ten times. There was no answer. Perhaps she had anothe
job.

I dialed Robert's number. Maybe he or his wife, if h
had one, could give me another number to call. I got

busy signal and hung up impatiently. As I was going to dial again, the phone rang.

"Florence?" an excited voice said. "I've found your mother. She's in Manhattan." It was Mr. Brooks.

I said: "I've also found her."

Speaking quickly, he said: "I just called your brother's wife. You know you have a brother?" He had gotten to the office early, seen my note, and had gone through the current directories. He had found all the Okuns in Manhattan and spoken to my sister-in-law. That was why I'd gotten a busy signal.

Oh, my God, I thought. *What has he done?* I didn't want to hurt his feelings; he was trying to help me, and he had been one of the very few people who ever *had* helped me. He was obviously deeply interested and genuinely excited about all the sudden developments. But if my mother's family did not know of my existence I wanted to shield her.

"Mr. Brooks," I said, a quiet fear creeping into my voice. "What did you say to her?"

"Well," he said, "I told her it was imperative that I locate her mother-in-law immediately on a matter of the utmost legal importance."

I closed my eyes. It was crucial that I make the initial contact. "What did you do?" I asked.

"She took my number and said she'd give it to your mother and have her call."

"What were you planning to do then?" I asked softly.

He said: "I was going to ask your mother whether she wants to see you."

"You were going to do what?"

"Florence?"

I told him quietly, patiently, that I appreciated with all my heart that he wanted to help me, but that I had to do this myself. I told him that my mother never had to see me again, but that I had questions and she was the only person who could answer them. I had no intention of intruding into her life, but I simply could not give her the option of *not* seeing me—not after all I'd been through.

"I only wanted to save you the aggravation," he said.

"I know, but no one can save me any aggravation. I've had it all. What else can happen? It's all over. Twenty years ago had I been lucky enough to meet you, you could have saved me a tremendous amount of heartache. But I've gone the whole route relatively alone, and I have to finish it alone. I'll make the contact. For my own feeling of pride in what I'm doing, and in myself, I must do it alone. I won't unload it on anybody else. I can handle it. If my mother tells me to go to hell I can handle it, and if she welcomes me with open arms I can handle it. If I could handle the last twenty years, I can manage whatever is coming in the next fifteen minutes."

He wished me good luck and asked me to call him later.

I jiggled the buttons on the telephone and got a fresh outside line. When my brother's wife picked up the phone, I said: "My name is Audrey. I'm from California and I think I'm a cousin of your husband's. I understand my lawyer, Mr. Brooks, just called you."

"Oh, yes," she said. "I'm terribly disturbed about that. I was wondering whether to call my mother-in-law immediately, or speak to Robert first."

"Don't call anyone," I said. "Please don't be upset. It's all quite simple." I told her an involved story I'd fabricated, concerning "my" grandmother and Hannah Cohen. I told her I was looking for Hannah Sweik Cohen's daughter.

"Oh, that's my husband's grandmother," she said, obviously relieved. "I remember the name Sweik. I'm so pleased it isn't something more serious."

"What I'd really like to do," I said, "is see your mother-in-law and any other relatives that I can—and be able to report back to my grandmother that I was able to make contact with her family. I have to be back in California in a few days."

"I'm *so* relieved," she said.

"I tried her at home and . . ."

"Oh, she's at work now."

I said: "Would you give me the number, please?"

Every moment mattered to me now. In a few hours I'd be able to reach her at her home, but I wanted it all over with. Fast. I felt like someone who has been traveling down a tortuous ski slope for a long time; I wanted to get to the bottom. Also, for a number of reasons it would be better to speak to her at her office than her home.

"Of course I can give you her number," my sister-in-law said. She told me my mother worked at a large department store, in the executive office.

It didn't occur to me to wait five minutes or until I could compose myself. What was the point? I wouldn't be more composed in one hour, ten hours, or ten years. I dialed each digit slowly, watching my fingers as they turned the dial clockwise to the top, all the way—each time slowly, crisply. *You're calling your mother. In another minute you'll hear your mother's voice.*

I coughed nervously to clear my throat, and waited for someone to pick up at the other end. I could feel my face flushing and I fought to keep the tears out of my voice. When the store operator answered, I said: "May I speak to Mrs. Okun, please, in the executive office?" My voice sounded calm; it had not broken.

"One moment." I heard the interoffice buzzer, lighter than the regular ring.

Then I heard, "Executive office. Mrs. Okun."

I was conscious of the way she enunciated each word. Her voice sounded—or did I imagine it?—similar to mine. I had often recorded my voice, to hear how I sang Italian love songs or the blues, and I could tell immediately that hers was a halftone down from my mezzo. But she enunciated her words in the same way.

I said: "You don't know me, Mrs. Okun, but I believe we're cousins." I heard my voice, out of the ghastly turmoil and near hysteria inside me, emerge cool and calm.

I could feel myself beginning to shake all over. Was this me? Or was someone else saying the words? "My name is Audrey Orenstein," I said, "and I'm quite sure we're related."

The woman said: "We don't have any Orensteins in the family."

"That's my married name," I said. My strength grew while I talked, but I knew I'd have to maintain absolute control if I was to carry this off without her suspecting for one moment what was going on inside me. "I'm from California and my grandmother came into the country between 1900 and 1910. She came with her cousin Hannah."

I heard my mother catch her breath. "That was my mother's name," she said tentatively.

I told her that my grandmother and her cousin were separated soon after they got to America, and that my grandmother had gone out West, where she married and had a family of her own. "She's very old and infirm now," I said, "but she still thinks nostalgically of Russia and of coming over on the boat with her cousin." I had not realized that I could maintain such outward composure. I knew all the details of my family so well that I had no trouble spinning out my tale. I didn't want to, but I knew it was necessary, and I kept hearing the words—calm and cool and pleasant—as if they were not mine. "They never saw each other again," I said. I paused for a moment. "Her cousin's name was Hannah Sweik."

"That was my mother!"

I felt horrible. My first contact with my mother was a lie. I had wanted to say, "Mother"—simply that. I wanted to say it now: "Mother." "Mother."

But I couldn't.

It would have been monstrous to announce, after all these years, "I'm your daughter." How could I possibly tell her that over the phone?

My well-rehearsed story was so plausible that she simply accepted it. *I'm lying to my mother.* I wanted to cry out.

I wanted to tell her: "I'm your daughter, Mother." But I heard myself still chatting on pleasantly into the phone about Cohens and more Cohens, while inside there was this shout: *Forgive me. I don't want to deceive you. I have to do it this way.*

She was saying: "Oh, I can't tell you how excited I am. I must call a cousin of mine—and yours, too, I guess—who keeps a family tree. I *must* see you. How long will you be here?"

"Just a few days. I'm here with my husband. We've got to go back to California soon." *I don't want to lie to you, mother.*

She said: "Let's set a time right now."

I said: "Would you meet me for lunch? Tomorrow . . ."

"I wouldn't think of meeting you for lunch," she said, interrupting me. "You and your husband must have dinner with us."

"No," I said softly. "It would be too much trouble for you." It was what I would have done. A hundred times I'd invited friends of ours from out of town to our apartment for dinner—just like that. They'd call from the airport, suddenly, and I'd go out to get them. They'd call from the city and I'd insist, and wouldn't take no's, that they come right over for dinner. But I couldn't go to her house. I couldn't possibly do that. But how could I get out of it?

"Look," she said. "I can't talk now because I'm at work and there are people in the office. Is there some place I can call you later? Are you staying at a hotel?"

I parried quickly. "No, I'm staying with relations of my husband," I said, and gave her my home phone number.

"Good," she said. "I'll call you as soon as I get home tonight and we'll arrange a time for you to come to dinner. I can't wait to meet you, Audrey."

When she hung up, I ran up to the Xerox room and broke down completely. Did I *really* have a mother? Had I *really* just spoken to her? I felt disembodied—as if I was on the outside looking in at my life. Tears poured down my cheeks and I pressed myself against the machine and sobbed uncontrollably.

I had always been angry when a friend or acquaintance assumed that at the end of my search I'd probably find someone reprehensible. The unwed mother who gives a child up for adoption, everyone assumes, is a slut. When I was a teen-ager, my adoptive parents had watched every move I made; they questioned me on my social life in detail; they censored my mail; they insulted my friends. I had long since realized they had been convinced that unless they hovered over me like constant *bodyguards*, I'd wind up as my mother had. Like mother like daughter. Heredity, for the adopted child, only works here; otherwise, in all other ways, the assumption is that the child owes everything to his environment, to his adoptive parents.

I had told my friends, "So what? I only want to find my parents; that's the important thing. I don't care if I find them in the gutter. They're what's behind the wall. They're part of the truth of who I am—and that's what I'm looking for. I'm looking for Anna Fisher."

Beyond that, though, I always had a firm belief that I would not find my mother in the gutter. There were qualities in me that I knew I would find in her and in my father—stubbornness, tenacity, pride, a love for music and theater and life. I had spoken to a perfectly lovely woman that morning who was my mother. She had sounded so warm and generous. She was outgoing and effervescent. She was so friendly, so kind.

All that afternoon I kept asking myself: "Did I really talk to my mother?" Yes, it *had* been her. I had done it.

And I had beaten the Greens and the Waxes and the sealed records. I had beaten the system; they had sealed my records, but they couldn't seal my mind. The satisfaction I had in this was all I really had—until I actually saw my mother. There was nothing more anyone could do to me, ever. All afternoon, intermittently, I cried and laughed and thought of what I would have to do next.

I cried on the subway, and the rush-hour crowd must have thought me stark mad. An elderly lady put her hand on my shoulder and said: "Can I help you, dear?"

"No," I said, smiling broadly. "I found my mother."

I cried in the butcher shop and the butcher, an old friend, said: "What's the matter? Are you all right?"

"I spoke to my mother," I told him.

He knew about my search. "She found her mother," he said excitedly to a customer, and the woman, seeing my joy, not knowing anything about the circumstances, put her arms around me and held me tight.

The phone was ringing when I entered my apartment a half hour later. I left the key in the door, dropped my packages, and ran into the bedroom.

"Hello, is this Audrey?" I knew the voice immediately.

"Yes," I said calmly.

"This is Florence Okun." *My God, if you only knew who you are talking to.* "You know, I've just called my cousin," she said, "and it's so strange: she keeps such a fantastic account of the family's activities but she's never heard of you or your family."

I said: "I never knew there was family in New York either." How could I keep so calm? I was holding the phone with my left hand and holding my left hand with my right hand to keep the receiver from knocking against my teeth.

We laughed and chatted and both sounded so self-assured, and it was all very light-headed and happy and otherworldly. I heard myself say: "I'd love to know something about your family."

"Oh, I have a wonderful family," she told me. She spoke glowingly about her son and daughter, about their achievements. Her son had majored in music and now was a performer.

I was starved for details and listened avidly as she went

on to tell me about her daughter's academic honors, her son's plans for the future, and how pleased she was with her daughter-in-law. "So you see," she said at length, "I have two lovely children."

I could tell she liked talking to me. I heard her say: "Our house was always filled with children and music."

It was almost too much to bear. I was sitting on the bed, the receiver pressed so close to my ear that my ear had grown flushed and hot. Outside the window, I could see a bright June sunset forming above the New Jersey Palisades. Already the pinks and blues, the gold and red were reflected on the Hudson River. It was all so unreal. I wanted to say: *I'm your daughter. You have three children.*

She was telling me about her brother, respected in his profession. My uncle. I felt sick deceiving her. She was being so open with me, so unsuspecting. *But I have a right to this information,* I thought. *It's my life history, too. This is my family. I have a right to know what my brother is, what my sister is; I have a right to know and feel proud of what an uncle of mine, my mother's brother, has achieved.*

Without resentment, but wistfully, I let my feelings speak. *We would have been close as mother and daughter —have liked each other. I know it. . . .* But I cut these thoughts off in a moment. What was, was. You couldn't go back.

"How proud you must be," I said.

"I am."

I once had Sodium Pentothal for an operation. When I came out of it, I heard everything through a mist. I felt that way now. Was I dreaming it all? It was too impossible: me talking to my mother, listening to her tell me about my brother and sister; she, chatting on as if we were old friends. The deception, the joy, the wistful sadness. And all the while I kept watching the bright orange crest of the sun slip down slowly into the Palisades:

now crimson purple, now pink and robin's-egg blue, as it vanished further below the slowly drifting clouds. Would she vanish too? Was she real?

"I have to work until five thirty," she said, "but I want you and your husband to come to dinner tomorrow night."

I asked: "Why did you move to New York last year? Didn't you like the suburbs?"

"Not really," she said. "But we made the decision for the children, while they were growing up, and now I want to be near the theater and the concert halls. I love Manhattan. Will tomorrow night be all right for you both?"

"Oh, by the way," I said, changing the subject again. "I've moved around the country quite a bit. Have you always lived in this area? Your accent isn't New York."

She laughed and said: "I've always tried to speak properly."

"Have you lived in New York all your life?" I pressed.

She paused. I could feel a painful silence. "Yes," she said hesitantly. She paused again. "Except for the time between when I was fourteen and seventeen. We lived in . . . in Philadelphia for a while. Look, I love having people for dinner and I wouldn't think of letting you leave town without coming over. We can try to figure out why the family tree isn't what it should be. I want you and your husband to come . . . let's make tomorrow definite."

"Well, we only have a few days . . . so why don't I simply meet you for lunch?"

"No, I'd really like to make it for dinner, when we'll have time to sit down for several hours and not be rushed. Anyway, my daughter is getting married and I'm going for fittings on my dress during lunch hours."

If her husband and family didn't know, it could blow her life apart to tell her in front of them, or anywhere near them. I *had* to see her alone. *Even if I go,* I thought rapidly, *maybe she looks like me; maybe she's a dead ringer for me and everyone will see it. There aren't so many years separating us.* The hypocrisy, the deception, were beyond my strength.

"Please say you'll come," she said.

"Can we have a drink together after you finish work?"

"That's silly. I only live a block from my office."

I said: "Perhaps a quick cup of coffee?" I was beginning to sound foolish. She couldn't help noticing if I kept this up.

"Absolutely not. I won't hear of anything else. You *must* come to dinner."

"Thank you," I said, "of course we'll come. You're very persuasive." I knew I couldn't push her further. Tomorrow I'd handle it. But no way, anyway, would I go to her house. "Why don't I meet you at your office and go home with you?"

She seemed puzzled by this, but we finally agreed, and I promised to meet her the next day at five thirty.

We had been talking for more than an hour. After I hung up I sat on the bed watching the last Monet-like moments of the sunset. The cars going back and forth on the George Washington Bridge turned on their lights, and the crisscross movement, back and forth across the river, was like the electrical current between two poles.

The fantasy of the evening turned into a long night, crowded with tossing and nightmares, until all disappeared in exhausted sleep.

Fourteen

Do you think you had a right to hunt down some woman just because she gave birth to you? What do you mean by heritage? You have a heritage from your adoptive parents.

—An adoptive parent

How am I going to tell her?

All that Friday, the twenty-sixth of June, two days after I'd found my grandparents' death certificates and learned my mother's married name and address, that question kept tormenting me. *What am I going to say? I'm your daughter?* Could I say it just like that? *I'm your daughter?*

Eleven thirty-five. It had been raining since early morning—a thick thunder-and-lightning summer storm. The rain slackened, the skies grew lighter for a moment, and then it was dark and wet again; the streets were in high flood, the windowpanes at my office were filled with droplets and little streams of rain. Here and there umbrellas that had been turned inside out by the winds lay crumpled against a wall or barricade.

I had brought a valise. I wanted to change before I

159

met my mother at five thirty. I had chosen a pale sea-green dress I'd designed myself, with a bow on each shoulder. It was soft-textured and went well, I thought, with the handbag I'd also made, with lavender and pale green grapes clustered at the sides and lavender and green velvet ribbons. I arose early and set my hair myself. When I saw the rain sweeping up and down the valley of the Hudson River, I had carefully packed everything I thought I'd need—cosmetics, perfume, a second pair of shoes, an extra pair of stockings, and my dress. Twice I went into the ladies' room to see if the rain had mussed my hair too badly. I looked in my valise to make absolutely sure I had brought everything I needed.

Why doesn't the storm stop?

I needed all my strength. The thunder and lightning and torrents of rain seemed to sap what little energy I had left. By noon I knew that my nerves would not hold. I began to remember nightmares I'd had that night, and on previous nights, that she was dead, or that she'd sensed who I was, that she'd fled. Over and over I rehearsed the words I knew I'd have to say: *I'm your daughter.* I had no idea how —or where—I was going to say them. I knew only two things with certainty: I would have to tell her and I would not go to her home.

I looked at my watch. Two fifteen. It had to be done. There was no question of my not going. I'd waited all my life. Within a few hours I'd see my mother. I wondered what she'd look like and what she'd say. Her voice had sounded so warm and generous on the phone; I knew I'd like her. But what would her reaction be? She had no idea *who* was meeting her. What would her reaction be when I told her: *I'm your daughter?* No matter. My long search was going to end. I looked at my watch again. Two twenty-two.

Stan had arranged to be at the house of a friend no three blocks from my mother's office. It was the closes place we'd been able to devise on such short notice; he knew I had to make this final move myself, but he wanted to be where I could reach him if he was needed.

If I don't get all the answers, I thought, *at least I'll get some of them. At least I'll see her.*

Three thirty-five. What could I say in the time it took to walk in the pouring rain the block from her office to her home? Could I possibly tell her that way? *I should have gone down lunch hour to see if there was a cocktail lounge nearby. I didn't want to get wet, and now I don't know where to take her.*

How can I tell her in the street? I can't tell her I'm her daughter on the street, in the rush-hour crowd, in the rain.

As it grew closer to five thirty, the weather grew worse. Now it was wholly black outside, and the rain came down in heavy sheets. I felt a deep depression settling in me. I desperately did not want to hurt her. I didn't know how well she'd learned to live with the whole series of events that must have surrounded my birth. I was almost, if not technically, born out of wedlock; my father might not have wanted the marriage. Had she ever thought of me? Did she regret having given me up? I knew she hadn't tried to find me, for one of my relatives—who all knew I was searching—would surely have told me. Did she want to forget, did she want to bury . . . *had* she virtually forgotten that she gave birth to a daughter forty years earlier? How could I tell her without hurting her? I didn't know her physical or mental condition.

I knew I had to get her into a seat somewhere, without explaining why.

I typed some correspondence and filed a half-dozen notes that my boss had left. Stan called. I told him it was awful, the waiting. He told me he could be wherever I was in less than ten minutes.

Four ten. I took my purse out of the bottom drawer of my desk and looked at the papers inside. I had brought with me my birth certificate, my Order of Adoption, my mother's birth certificate, her wedding license, and the death certificates of my two grandparents. I laid them out on the desk and scanned them again.

Everything confirmed everything else.

At four twenty I went in to get dressed. When I came out my friends in the office gathered around me. One of them said my eyes were red and swollen. Another put her hand on my shoulder; she felt the shaking and told me everything would be all right. I could feel a slow tremor working its way through my whole body. My arms wouldn't stay still.

I took a pocket mirror out of my purse and saw that my eyes were like red balloons. I'd brought some boric acid solution with me, and after I'd washed my eyes for a few moments, the swelling went down. My friends began to become terribly concerned about me. The shaking had not stopped, I'd gone ghostly pale, and I could hardly stand. I never take pills, but I knew that this time I couldn't go through with it without some help. Everyone hunted throughout the offices, and finally they found a potent tranquilizer. I took it at once.

Within moments my arms stopped shaking. One of us would have to be calm and rational, I thought. At least I knew what I was getting into. What would she know? She thought she was going to meet a distant cousin from California. She couldn't possibly be prepared for what would take place. At all cost, I *had* to remain calm.

I left the office at four forty-five. My friends came to the door with me, wished me well, and assured me my mother would be glad to see me. I'm always late for everything, and this time I was determined to be early. I tried to smile. I could only say "thank you" in a husky voice and then hurry out.

I had so much wanted to look pretty, but the rain seemed only to increase as I ran out to hail a cab; I was afraid that despite my raincoat and plastic rain bonnet, I'd look a mess by the time I saw her. In the cab I realized that

though my arms were calm, my legs were still shaking. I
kept thinking: *How do I say, I'm your daughter. How do
I say the words? And where?*

I told the cab driver: "Please hurry. But please be careful." *Don't let anything happen to me before I see my
mother.* I looked at my face in a hand mirror. My eyes were
still red and a little swollen. I put on dark glasses.

It was good that I'd left early. We were in the midst of
rush-hour traffic and for long minutes we'd stay in one
place, listening to the incessant honking, watching the
windshield wipers snap back and forth, back and forth.
How do I say it?

I had to talk to someone or I'd burst. "I'm going to see
my mother," I said out loud, "for the first time in my life."

The cab driver, a burly man with a peaked cap flat on
his head, turned around, looked at me, and said: "Waddaya
mean yer gonna see your mother for the first time?"

I leaned forward. "I was adopted. I've looked for her
all my life, and only found her yesterday. She doesn't know
I'm coming; she doesn't know I'm her daughter."

When we stopped in another traffic jam a few moments
later, he turned around again, looked at me, and could
only shake his head. *What will she look like? What will
she say? Will she be able to take the shock?* I noticed that
my hands were gripping the door handle with a death-
hold; they were like ice.

The cab driver said: "That's some story, lady. I've
heard lotsa stories, but that's *some* story."

In a few more minutes we were there. As I handed the
driver his money, he turned around again, saying in a
husky voice: "Good luck, honey."

"Thanks," I said. "I'll need it."

With the rain bonnet and dark glasses obscuring my face,
I walked into the store, found an information booth, and
asked where the executive offices were. Upstairs I asked
the way to Mrs. Okun's office.

"Through that door," a clerk said. "Do you have an appointment?"

I said: "She's expecting me."

I pushed the door and, following it as it swung inward, thought, *This is it*.

The first thing I saw were my mother's legs; they were plump. She was bending over some files and as I saw her I thought, *That's what I'm going to look like in seventeen years*. She was small, like me—but heavier: as I'd be if I didn't eat lettuce.

She turned around.

I have never known nor will I ever feel again a wave of happiness such as I did the moment I first saw my mother. She was no longer a dream, an idea, a figment of my imagination; she was not an image conjured up by my longing, a shadow haunting my sleep. My mother was real.

In an instant I took in every feature of her face: her eyes, her high cheekbones, a certain curve of her ears, the precise shape of her nose, her expression. Only her mouth was different, and she was heavier: otherwise we might have been sisters. Even her hair was dark, my natural color; the shape of the face and the animation in her eyes were the same as mine. She was not pretty, not glamorous —nor am I.

Suddenly the anguish of years fell away.

I had grown so used to the heaviness in my heart, had lived with the pain for so long, that when it fell away I felt light and free.

She said to me: "Are you Audrey?"

I said: "Yes, I am."

"Would you mind waiting a moment, dear?" she asked.

A moment? I had an impulse to laugh hysterically. From behind my dark glasses, from under my hoodlike rain bonnet, I peered out at her. I memorized every line of her face. *A moment!* I'd waited years, waited in courts and lawyers' offices, waited while strangers scratched their memories, waited for names to appear in dry old telephone directories. *Yes, I could wait a moment longer. Now, mother, I can wait.* "No," I said. "Of course I don't mind waiting."

Maybe it was the drug I'd taken. I felt light. I sat in the outer office, waiting for my mother to come out, and thought of the countless hours I had spent at my other mother's kidney-shaped dressing table with the three mirrors, looking at all those family pictures, trying desperately to find a nose or eye or ear among the hundreds of old photographs that reminded *me* of *me. How do I tell her?* There was so very much I wanted to say to her; I wanted to tell her how happy I was, just seeing her, just talking to her—but I couldn't think of the right first words.

I loved the way she looked. She *was* my mother. The real shock was seeing that she wasn't seventeen years old, as I had been imagining her; but there was absolutely no doubt in my mind who she was.

In a few moments she came out, carrying her umbrella and saying, "I'm ready."

I'm not, I thought. I had an intense desire to touch her.

Soon we were in the elevator making idle conversation. I could scarcely hear anything she said. I wanted to take off my dark glasses but did not. I knew I couldn't tell her here, in a crowded elevator. But where? We were nearing the first floor and I knew we'd only have a block before we reached her house. I had to find a way to stop, and to stop her.

Outside, the storm had grown heavier. We looked at each other and shook our heads. She opened her umbrella; I opened mine.

We started walking up the block. Thoughts crowded my mind as I searched for a way out of the trap. *I've got to stop her. I can't go to her home.* I turned to her and started to speak but did not.

She said something about the rain, something about a casserole in the oven, something about having gone home lunchtime to prepare something. I heard her words but

I couldn't catch hold of them. My mind was working too fast.

We had gone a block when I took a quick breath and said: "I wonder if we could go somewhere for coffee before we go to your house."

She gave me a curious look and said: "We could have it at my home."

I said, "There's something I'd like to ask you about both our families that . . . that really doesn't concern your husband or mine. So could we just have a few moments together—before we go to your house? Please?"

She looked at me strangely again, skeptically, and said: "Of course. If you want to. There's a coffee shop down the block."

We walked toward it, saying nothing now. We closed our umbrellas, went in, walked down past the counter, and found a table in the back. In a moment we were seated.

She looked at me expectantly.

I wanted desperately to say something to her, anything. A full minute or two went by. I could tell that the tranquilizer had stopped working. She kept looking at me; I still had on my dark glasses and hooded rain bonnet, and peered out from under them at her.

I said: "I don't know how . . . to begin."

I choked up. I didn't want to cry. *Oh God, don't let me break down and cry.*

She said nothing. I *couldn't* tell her; the words would not come out of my mouth. I opened my purse quickly, fumbled in it, looked down, and took out my birth certificate. I handed the paper across the table to her. Then I took out the Order of Adoption, her birth certificate, her marriage license, and then the two death certificates of Moishe Cohen and Hannah Zweick Cohen. One by one I handed them to her.

Neither of us said a word. Her face, looking briefly at the birth certificate and then toward me, was blank. I removed my rain bonnet, folded it, and laid it on the table.

I removed my dark glasses and put them in my purse. I looked constantly at her face. It was a mask.

She took all the papers in her hands now and, very casually, very quickly flipped through them with her fingers, glancing briefly at each one. Then she put them down.

A stranger would have been more interested in reading them. My mother *knew* the contents.

I said: "I want you to know that I don't have any desire to intrude in your life but . . ."

She looked directly at me and, without changing her expression, said: "What is this?"

I said quietly: "I've spent the last twenty years looking for you." I looked at her. The cousin who had been so delighted to take a cousin home to dinner had vanished. Her expression had become cool, veiled. "It should be obvious that I don't want to intrude in your life or I would have gone right to your home. But I've been searching all my life, my whole life, and there are questions that I have that only two people in the world can answer—you and my father."

She looked directly at me, and without a moment's hesitation said: "I believe you're mistaken. I'm not the person you're looking for."

Did she really say that?

Was it possible?

She took out a cigarette, lit it, and began to smoke rapidly. The waitress standing beside our table asked us impatiently what we wanted to order. We both said "coffee" at the same time.

Did she really say that?

I told her I had been adopted as a baby. I felt ridiculous. I told her there were many things in my nature that I could in no way attribute to my environment.

"I've always felt it was a person's environment that made them what they are," she said.

"It's because I'm so different genetically from my

adoptive parents . . . this above all led me to search for my father—and for you."

"I'm terribly sorry," she said, "but I'm really not the person you're looking for." She lit another cigarette.

I looked at her but said nothing. She saw I was not going to drop it.

She asked: "Why is this so important to you? It's not the mother who bears you," she said, "but the one who brings you up who counts." *That* from my mother, too. Did she *really* believe it? Or was it a bitter, but necessary, rationalization for what she had done?

"I didn't look only for my mother and my father. I looked for the truth. I've been lied to all my life. I have a right to the truth and there are only two people in the world who can give it to me. Until I find my father, there's only you. Nobody else."

She must *find it in her heart to tell me.*

She finished her fourth or fifth cigarette and ground it into an ashtray.

"The truth," I said softly, "that's all I want from you. Nothing else. I don't want to be included in your life. That would be nice, but if it's not possible, it's not possible; I have a good life. But I must have the answers. I want to know who my father was. I want to know why I was given up for adoption. I want to know who you are. I want to know what you are. I want to know who and what my grandparents were." I was speaking in a low, soft tone. I did not want to badger her like this. I had not wanted to badger Dr. Green or Mr. Wax or Wax's widow. "I have a child," I said, "and I have a responsibility to pass this information on to him, just as you have to pass it on to me. I must have these answers—for my peace of mind. I've earned the answers."

She said: "I wish I could help you but I can't."

I said: "You can if you want to."

She asked me to tell her something about myself, what I did.

I told her that I lived in New York, not California; that I simply couldn't tell her on the phone who I was. "The very fact that I called my brother's wife and gave her the same story should prove to you that I don't wish to hurt you." I told her why I didn't want to come to her house. "I couldn't sit at your table," I said, "and look at your husband—not knowing if he knew—and pretend to be your cousin. When I'm your child."

She lit another cigarette and began to ask me questions —who I was, what I'd done with my life.

It was bizarre. Either she *was* my mother or she wasn't my mother. If she wasn't, why would she ask all these questions? Why would she be interested?

I had seen nothing but a studied calm in her eyes. She sat there looking at *me* with *my* face. If she was bluffing, no one had ever done it better. But was it possible, even remotely possible, that she *wasn't* my mother?

I had checked and checked—a hundred times—those documents that now lay before her on the table, those papers she had flipped through so casually. Could there be any doubt whatsoever that the woman before me, who looked like me and spoke like me, was not Florence Cohen, the daughter of Morris and Hannah Sweik Cohen, the wife of Frederick Fisher? Was it remotely possible that some false names were placed on my birth certificate, and that I had checked out a family for twenty years that was no more mine than a stranger's?

I decided to answer her questions.

I told her I'd always had a passion for reading; I told her I loved music and the arts and the theater, that I'd always been something of a dreamer. I told her I loved to make things with my hands, and that I'd been taking music lessons and voice lessons and that I sang in a semi-professional chorus. "I love to sing," I told her, "and to play the piano. I've even taught myself several languages."

She looked at me and for a moment I thought—or I may have imagined it—that a glimmer came into her eyes.

For a moment they seemed not so masked, so cool. Was it pride? Did she recognize in my face and my loves something of her own? Did she see in my interests something that might have been born in her? She kept smoking incessantly, one cigarette after the other, lighting one with the other.

She casually picked up the documents again, glanced through them, and said: "I *couldn't* be the person you're looking for; I was born in 1920."

She flipped them until she came to Hannah Cohen's death certificate. "My mother's name was spelled Z-w-e-ik," she said, pronouncing the word carefully. "Without the *c*.

"I really wish I could help you," she said quickly, "but I can't."

I took a deep breath now. I had wanted to spare her. I saw no reason to hurt her. All I wanted, for once, was the truth. I was getting lies again—and now from *her*. *Am I asking you for so much?* I thought. *You want to know about my life. All right. I'm going to let you know about my life. I love you; you're my mother, but . . .*

And then, blow by blow, without embellishment, I told her what my life had been as a child.

"And still," I said quietly, when I had finished, "that is not the reason I looked. I don't resent *you* because of it, I looked because there was a closed door that I had to open. Only you have the key."

I had no more strength. I had nothing else to say.

She had listened to every word; she had looked at the documents; she had watched me constantly, looking down only now and then at her cigarette or at her hands— chubby little hands, like mine.

I can be just as cool when I have to. *"Il sangue chiama,"* the Italians say. Blood calls blood. Maybe not. I can be cool—but could I deny my own child?

I was numb. I could go on no longer. I gave an enormous sigh and settled back in my chair. *Basta*. Enough.

She put out her last cigarette, stood up, and said for the third time: "I'm sorry, I'm not the person you're looking for." *She never said, "I'm not your mother."*

I saw, as she picked up the check for the two cups of coffee we hadn't touched, that her hands were shaking now. I had wanted to get to the check first, but I couldn't move my arms.

She took out her change. I thought, *Let your mother buy you a cup of coffee, Florence.* Then she knocked over the ashtray, did not turn back, and hurried out.

I sat at the table unable to move. *Well,* I thought, *there goes my mother.*

I ordered a cup of tea but didn't drink it. I looked at the little pile of documents on the table, where my mother had left them. I sat for half an hour, unable to move, unable, really, to think. Finally I tried to compose myself. Stan was waiting and he'd be worried. I reached across the table, took the papers in my hand, and slowly put them back in my purse. As I got up to leave I noticed the fallen ashtray and bent down to pick it up.

On the floor, next to the ashtray, was something black. I stared at it.

She had dropped her wallet.

It was too late to go after her, and I certainly didn't want to leave it with the people at the luncheonette. I *couldn't* bring it to her home. So I took it with me.

The first thing I said to my husband was: "She said, 'I'm not the person you're looking for.' "

I took her wallet out of my purse and placed it on the table.

"What's that?" Stan asked.

"Her wallet. She dropped it."

He asked: "Have you looked in it?"

"No," I said. I was obsessed with privacy. I didn't even glance at the other side of my husband's postcards.

But I knew I had to see what was in this wallet. *Maybe she's not your mother,* I thought. *It's not possible, but she*

did say she was born in a different year. Inside the wallet
would I find the final proof? Stan looked at me when I
picked it up, and nodded.

The first item I saw was her driver's license. It gave
her correct day of birth and the year was the same as that
on her birth certificate. There was a signature. I took the
documents out from my purse, laid them on the table, and
fetched out one I was searching for.

Her signature, forty years later, was nearly identical
with that on the wedding license.

Fifteen

I was overwhelmed with desire to keep my baby after birth but they kept repeating all the reasons why it was mature to give her up, that I would forget. No one told me I'd have these feelings all my life.
                                        —A natural mother

I had broken part of the veil of secrecy. I had seen my mother and I had spoken to her. I knew where she was and, to a certain extent, who she was. I did not know precisely why she had refused to acknowledge what we were to each other. Was it guilt? Or did she think once she'd closed the door, that was that?

I had a choice—or, rather, several choices. I could decide that she had her chance and I had my chance, and it was not to be: we need never see each other again. For whatever reason, she did not want to see me.

I might also choose to press the issue now—to challenge her as, in my urgency, I had challenged others in the past. I could call her; I could write her letters.

Or I could wait, and hope she would come to me.

Part of my choice, I knew, would depend upon what,

emotionally, I was able to do—and what I needed to do. I did not want to hurt my mother; I still wanted to protect her. She must have had her reasons for refusing to admit what was so obvious. *It all must pain her very deeply,* I thought.

That night I made a decision.

She now knew where to find *me.* I decided to give her two months, until the end of the summer, to contact me. If she would not tell me by then, there were other people who would. I had not said to her, "Tell me or I'll tell them." *She looks like me,* I thought, *but if she can walk away from this without telling me, she isn't anything like me.* I could afford to give her that long to come to me, but I would not lose one-half of my life and come up with a zero.

There was still the wallet.

In it I had found photographs of my grandparents, and of my brother and sister. I looked at the young man and young woman for a long time; I thought I'd like to know them. They did not resemble my mother in any way. I was her image. There were also a dozen credit cards in the wallet and other important documents. I knew my mother would be extremely upset when she missed it. But because of my decision I did not want to return it to her myself.

On Monday morning I asked one of my closest friends to call my mother. "Please just tell her that late this afternoon, by messenger, I'm sending her her wallet. I don't want her to worry."

All weekend I had given the matter constant thought. It hurt me, but I had finally decided what I must do. I Xeroxed the detailed diary I'd made covering the entire search; the last fifteen months were fully documented.

Then I typed out this letter. It had no salutation.

"To deny your identity could, in effect, send me on a search that would last my entire life for a nonexistent

Florence Cohen. There was no doubt in my mind before we met. Seeing and speaking with you merely confirmed what the documents prove.

"If you know yourself, then you must know that I am neither capable of causing you harm nor of disrupting your present life.

"Many years ago I read a poem, the lines of which have been engraved in my soul:

> *Oh, why does the wind blow upon me so wild?*
> *Is it because I'm nobody's child?*

"My search has not only been for you and Frederick Fisher but for the truth that has always been denied me—and which, because of that denial, I value above all else. You have it in your power to give me the truth . . . but you must do as your instinct guides.

Florence"

I wrapped the letter, the diary, and the wallet carefully, and addressed it to Florence Okun. When the messenger came, I described my mother to him and said, "Be sure, be absolutely sure you give this to her and to nobody else. In fact, call me when you get there, when you've actually seen the woman. Describe her to me, and then I'll tell you whether or not to give her the package."

An hour later he called me, said he'd seen her, and described her to me. It was my mother. I told him he could give her the packet.

That night I felt calm inside. I had looked at my mother, and I had spoken to her. She had looked at me with eyes as nearsighted as mine; had spoken to me with my voice. And then she had said she wasn't the person I was looking for. Well, I was still ahead of the game: I had an image of her inside me, for the first time in my life, and I cherished that image.

I had hoped it would all be easier, but I had done

what I had set out to do—knowing there was no sure paradise at the end of the trail. The worst had happened and now it was over. I was disappointed—but I knew it was only a matter of time before I got all the answers. I felt positive and good—and, for the first time in many weeks, I slept dreamlessly and deep.

When I got to the office on Tuesday morning, there was a message that someone had called me but left no name; the operator thought it might be one of my friends.

I was busy with some correspondence when the phone rang. I picked it up, said hello, tucked it between my shoulder and my chin, and heard: "I can't talk." The voice was thin and choked up. "Can I . . . see you?"

I recognized her at once and asked where she'd like to meet.

"I . . . don't know." Listening to that familiar voice, hearing it hesitate and then press on against all that must be keeping it from speaking, tore me apart.

"Would you like to come to my home?" I asked.

"No, no," she said.

I thought for a moment, then we arranged to meet at six o'clock at the Beekman Tower. It would be quiet there; perhaps we could talk.

I left the office as soon as I could, went home, showered, and lay down for a long rest. I got up about four, changed into fresh clothes, and made myself up carefully. As I drove downtown in a taxi, I realized I was not nearly as nervous as I had been on our first meeting; just seeing her had stilled the mountain of turbulence in me. I hadn't sought acceptance and I didn't feel that I had been rejected. I felt relatively calm. I had heard in her voice a readiness to talk.

I took the elevator to the top of the building. There is an unenclosed outdoor patio surrounding the lounge, and since it was a beautiful June evening I decided to take one of the outdoor tables, where we could look out over

e city and talk quietly. I sat facing east, so I would see my
other when she entered.

She was no more than a few minutes late, but apologized
t once, saying the traffic had delayed her.

She was very clean, very neat, very freshly made up—
nd very, very nervous. She had on a simple, pretty brown,
hite, and black print dress, and every hair was carefully
a place. I knew she must have gone home to change as
had. She sat down, looked carefully at me, and tried to
peak. I could see that she was terribly upset but that she
asn't going to cry; her mask was gone, but she had poise
nough to contain herself. I was proud of her. She faltered
nd tried again. "I . . . I just don't know . . . where to
egin," she said. "I . . . don't know *how* to begin."

I can't remember what I said. I know only that I wanted
ery much to put her at her ease and that I think I did.
he waitress came over and we gave our orders for
rinks.

My mother did not take her eyes off me. "When I saw
he birth certificate," she said, hesitantly, "I felt like a
. . like a building had caved in on me."

"I know," I said softly.

"You see, I had buried it for all these years. It had been
very painful experience in my life." Her voice was low
ut firm now. Her lips opened in a small smile as she
old me she'd never lost anything in her life; dropping her
allet, she implied, may have been the only way she
ould tell me. "I went through the entire weekend in a
ance." She paused. I could see that she was being ex-
remely careful not to solicit my sympathy for what she
ad done. "Forgive me for saying what I did," she said
imply. "I knew you *knew*. I . . . I didn't know what to
ay."

"You did beautifully," I said. I wanted to let her know
hat I had understood. I saw her hand reach out across
he table toward me—and then pull back and rest on the
ablecloth.

We spoke for a few moments, and then she began to tell me what I had always wanted to know. That night I met *my mother*—and my past. And the dark veil began to fall away.

She had been about fourteen when her family moved to Philadelphia, to live at the Walnut Street address. In those days, she told me, there was much less formal dating, but everyone would gather at someone's house to spend the evening talking, singing, and playing the piano; they weren't parties but informal gatherings. My mother had a piano and played well, so the gatherings were often at her house. In the summer before I was born, one of the neighborhood boys who came to the gatherings was Fred Fisher. "He was handsome," she said. "He was on his own, working as a law clerk—and I fell in love as one does only at sixteen."

She paused, touched my hand, and continued. "Your father had auburn hair, a face full of freckles and laughing blue-gray eyes." *My son's eyes.* "Although we were close in age, he seemed much older. He was sophisticated and charming, perhaps because of his beautiful voice, so deep and resonant. He was my first love—and you were a child of that love." She went on. "Those were Depression years. Your grandfather's business failed and we were forced to return to New York. Fred and I thought we were seeing each other for the last time . . . that was why things happened as they did."

Mother became less nervous as she talked. Truth is cleansing and her words began to flow freely. I listened intently, each word filling the void I had lived with for so long. Suddenly a date, a place, or a street address was mentioned, and I would remember how once it had been nothing more than an entry on a page. Now it was invested with meaning.

Now and then there was pain in her voice, but as more and more of the details came out, I realized that she might never have confided in anyone before—and that talking to e might be her first release from the prison of her silence.

By mid-autumn she realized she was pregnant. She and
y father were now separated by a hundred miles and as
e months went on she became more and more desperate.
[y mother is proud and tried to resolve her situation
ithout telling my father. She didn't want to be married
ider those circumstances. By January she had no choice.
ie wrote to a friend asking her to contact my father.
hey were married at a simple wedding in Philadelphia
ree months before I was born. My mother had just
rned seventeen, my father was eighteen. His father made
e arrangements and attended the wedding. They rented
room at the Chestnut Street address listed on their mar-
age certificate. The landlady's memory simply had been
ulty.

My maternal grandparents knew nothing of the wedding
itil it was over. When they were told, my grandmother
:came hysterical; my father was not the son-in-law she
id envisioned for her daughter.

As the weeks moved on, the pressures grew. My father
st his job and could not find another. The little cash
ey'd been given as wedding presents was exhausted and
y mother's father came to Philadelphia to take her back
New York. My father followed her but her family would
ot permit him to see her. Finally, when he found a way,
y grandmother threw him out. She could not bear the
ght of my mother, called her vile names, and kept shout-
g: "You're no child of mine!"

My mother went on, painfully now. "So a friend of my
other's at 695 Broadway took me in, and for the last
onths nobody saw me. I supported myself by doing
usework for them."

When her time came the woman with whom she lived
ok her to the hospital. My grandparents refused to visit
r and she was told I was born dead. For four days she
lieved this, while my grandmother and her friend tried
give me away without going through legal channels.

Only when they were told that the mother's signature wa
necessary did they finally tell her I was alive.

Dr. Green and my grandmother's friend told mothe
there was a childless couple who wanted to adopt a baby
"They're young, rich, and well-educated," she was tol
My grandmother sent a message that if she gave me u
for adoption she could come home; otherwise, since sh
was a minor, they would place her in a home for waywar
girls after they annulled the marriage.

"I was seventeen, alone, and terribly frightened," sh
said, putting her hand across the table to finally touch an
hold mine.

She had agreed to the adoption and was never per
mitted to see me. My adoptive parents took me hom
from the hospital. She had never physically seen me unti
four days ago, when I walked into her office.

We were no longer strangers now, as she filled in thes
details of my heritage. No, she hadn't named me and ha
no idea where the name Anna had come from. She smile
as she said: "I couldn't possibly have named you that
Adrianne, perhaps, if I had wanted a name beginning witl
A—but never Anna." More than thirty-five years earlie
I had first seen that name, Anna Fisher, on a certificate o
adoption. Somewhere between the birth certificate, whic
listed me as "Baby Fisher," and the Order of Adoption
naming me "Florence," "Anna" had come and gone
Perhaps some nurse in the hospital, feeling "Baby Fisher
too anonymous, had named me Anna out of kindness
Strangely, the name became dearer to me now that
knew it belonged to that limbo I had lived with so long.

I told my mother about Dr. Green and she nodded sev
eral times while I talked. "He knew I was married," sh
said, "and that I'd had to get married. He must hav
thought that because I had become pregnant before
was married I must be very free. 'Good Jewish girls' o
sixteen or seventeen didn't get pregnant in those days
When I went to his office for my post-partum examina

tion," she said, "he . . . he tried . . . I had to run out of there . . . It was horrible."

I realized that must have been the reason for his intense shock at seeing me. I was in my early twenties, and at that time looked very much like my mother had at eighteen. He had blanched when he saw me; suddenly I *was* my mother—and she had rejected him. His savage outburst had been his revenge.

We had decided to stay together for only an hour, but as we began to talk the time evaporated. She told me about her childhood, how she'd loved to act, how she'd been in all the school plays. Her father had loved the arts, and frequently took her to the ballet, the opera, the theater; but her mother never seemed to have liked her—and from the time of her marriage right up to her recent death, my grandmother had continued to taunt my mother about what she had done. I felt a tremendous sense of triumph over Hannah Sweik Cohen, who appeared to have been the cause of all that happened—and whose name had led me to this moment.

It had taken my mother ten years to get back into life after I was born, and even when she remarried, she could only tell her new husband that she had once been married and that the marriage had been annulled. She could not bring herself to say, I gave my baby away, and so told him that her child had been born *dead*.

I shuddered at the word.

After my mother's second marriage she had a child who *was* born dead. This time my grandmother visited her at the hospital to tell her she had finally "paid" for what she had done.

My mother said she had been active socially all her life but had always avoided the limelight—perhaps because she feared discovery. Perhaps now she could tell her husband and her children; perhaps . . . but she would have to wait, and think it out.

Now and again she would reach across the table to

touch my hand as she talked. What great compassion and overwhelming love I had for her. I reluctantly reminded her that the family might be worried about her; I didn't want her to have any pressure at home. But she said she'd told them she was going shopping; she could stay a little longer without arousing alarm. It was a gorgeous June evening—calm and pleasantly warm—and I looked over now and then to the west, where the sun was beginning to set.

We moved off onto other subjects, how we had both read and loved Dumas and Hugo as little girls, *Anna Karenina* and *Wuthering Heights*—how we both loved music, particularly the piano. We listened hungrily to one another, peering at each other—she saying suddenly, "Your mouth is just like my brother's but the rest of your face is mine."

When she saw the handbag I carried, she said: "You know, I make bags."

I said: "I made this one—and I make hats also."

Softly she said: "Yes, I make hats, too." She told me that she'd often work at night when she couldn't sleep.

Once she said: "Tell me everything about your childhood, even the things you said . . . on Friday."

"Why repeat them?" I said quietly. "They happened a long time ago—and they're over now."

"Don't hate me," she said.

"How could I ever hate you?" I asked. "You're my mother."

We were together for more than three hours. The sun was below the line of the buildings now, and I could only see its crimson glow at the base of the sky. We had tried to cram a lifetime into one evening. There was still so much unsaid, but I was finally through the looking-glass; my questions were answered. Several times my mother arose to go, looked at me, and sat down again.

Finally we could push back the hours no longer. It had grown dark and my mother had to leave. We got up together and then she moved around the table to take my arm. I told her of my decision—that I'd never call her; she would have to call me. She said nothing. We walked toward the elevator together, arm in arm, unable to resist the temptation to touch each other, as we had reached out all evening, in our words, with our hands, to touch each other's mind and heart. In the elevator, as we stood together silently, I thought, with a bittersweet pang, how sad it was that we should be meeting this late, that we had missed a lifetime of love. We kept looking at each other closely in the elevator, but said nothing.

It was dark outside, and we walked slowly to the corner, arm in arm, holding hands tightly, walking close. I realized, suddenly, that I didn't want to prolong the evening; I didn't know how much longer I would be able to stand it. I had been prepared to talk to her for an hour, but not for us to feel so comfortable with each other, to find so much in common, to speak so profoundly for so long. She was my mother, my *real* mother, and for this evening—if never again—we had found each other, as if the cord had never been cut, the papers never signed.

But the evening had to end, and I wanted it to end soon—and at the same time didn't want it to end at all.

Before she got into a taxi, my mother put her arms around me and held me very close for several long moments. "Let's not say good-bye," she said softly.

I couldn't say a word. She looked at me through the window of the cab; I kept looking at her. Then I watched the cab drive off up First Avenue. I watched until it got to the corner, turned, and suddenly went out of sight. I had on a pink dress with puffed sleeves. It was a little girl's dress. I stood looking at the corner around which my mother's cab had just disappeared.

Whether we had a relationship or not wasn't important at the moment. It would be wonderful if we could build one; the lovely person I found at the end of my search made every moment of the twenty years worthwhile. The questions, the secrets, the mysteries that had gnawed at me since childhood were gone. I was connected to this woman, and linked to a past, to a whole world of people who in some way shared my . . . yes, my blood, my ancestry, and I felt more strength for the future. Inside me, that great void was filled. Head and heart—and something so palpable as blood: all felt stronger than they'd ever felt before. The evening had been like looking in a mirror—and seeing a reflection for the first time.

She had not wanted to leave me; I knew that. How bittersweet was the joy of finding her, how sad the separation.

I felt two years old. There on the corner I said to no one at all: *"I want my mother."*

But I wasn't two. I was an adult. A mother myself.

I turned and went home.

Sixteen

Whenever and wherever adoption can be avoided, and the natural mother and her baby kept together, this is without a doubt the better choice from the point of view of the psychological consequences.

> —Dr. Zellig Bach
> Clinical Psychologist

In all the years of my childhood and search, I had never thought of adoption in relation to anyone but myself. I was unaware of other adoptees engaged in a similar pursuit—of an adoption "problem."

It was a blustery night in January, the winter after I found my mother. The past months had been good ones. Everything seemed to be settling inside me. My defiance of a law I considered unjust had proved fruitful. I reveled in having beaten the sealed records and was convinced I would make it a doubleheader by finding my father. I had searched again for my father, and was determined to continue in the spring, when the weather was warmer.

My job at the Philharmonic was over. I was no longer working—I was enjoying the freedom to explore my many interests, and especially enjoying my peace of mind. I caught up on my reading, listened to music, dabbled in gourmet cooking, and Stan and I went to the theater regularly.

However, at that moment I was seated at the piano in a determined attempt to master Debussy. And Debussy was winning. Stan turned on the TV and suddenly I heard the words, "Baby Lenore," "Adoption," "Save Baby Lenore." A moment later the picture of a baby flashed on the screen and I began to listen avidly to the last words of an editorial decrying the "unfortunate fact" that a natural mother was fighting to get her baby back from its adoptive parents.

"What are they doing?" I said to Stan.

For a fleeting moment *I* was that baby. *My* chance to stay with *my* real mother was being taken away.

So profoundly was I affected by the Baby Lenore case that during the following days I bought every newspaper on the stands and listened to all the news broadcasts.

As I devoured every scrap of information I could find about the case I realized that the adoptive parents were being quoted and applauded everywhere. Nowhere had I seen or heard a word of compassion for the natural mother. I was mystified. The trial judge had decided that the best interests of the child would be served by returning her to her natural mother, a mother whom he had found to be fit, competent, and able to raise her baby. I located a copy of the *Law Journal* in which his decision was printed, and as I slowly pored over the facts my amazement grew. The child, it turned out, had *never* been legally adopted. Why, then, had she been referred to in the media as the "adopted child"? She had been in the prospective adoptive home only *five* days when the natural mother contacted the agency to rescind her surrender. The prospective parents must have known within three months, for that's when the case went to court.

Why hadn't they given her back!

The case haunted me. Assemblymen crying, "We don't want any more Baby Lenores," were trying to pass legislation on the heat of a case that I felt had been grossly misreported to the public. The new "thirty-day surrender bill" would give the natural mother only thirty days after she signed the surrender to alter her decision; I checked and saw that the present law gave her six months. That seemed fair. Fair to the adoptive parents, fair to the natural mother, fair to the child. Any girl who has gone through the trauma of an out-of-wedlock pregnancy *must* have time to regain her strength, time to fully consider all the consequences of her decision. But the thirty-day bill seemed punitive and inhumane, and I was saddened to think that society didn't realize that to punish the mother was also to punish the child.

My mind was awhirl. What was the whole truth—not simply in my case, or that of "Baby Lenore"—but about the institution of adoption itself?

Like a homing pigeon, I returned to the library. H. David Kirk, a sociologist and adoptive parent of four, had written a book called *Shared Fate*. Fascinated by his theories I read it through twice. I discovered Margaret Kornitzer's fine *Adoption and Family Life* and Jean Paton's thoughtful and sensitive *Orphan Voyage*. Miss Paton, a social worker, had been adopted twice as a young child. She saw in the search for natural parents a close parallel to the myth of Oedipus Rex, who asks that perennial question: "Who Am I?" His answer to that question, Miss Paton pointed out, was dependent upon knowing "the roots which grew to Oedipus."

As I studied these and many other technical books on the subject, I realized that I had viewed adoption emotionally and privately. I had reached many of the same conclusions these writers had, but they brought the entire adoption picture into focus for me, objectified and clarified it—showed me adoption extended beyond the perimeters of my own existence.

I also began to see adoption as a problem "in time." When I was a child, most parents failed to tell their children they were adopted; it was a dark secret. Today, experts favored early disclosure. This was certainly an improvement. But once adoptive parents had admitted the existence of two other people in their children's lives, did they expect their children to become instant amnesiacs? Mere disclosure still did not resolve some of the findings in recent studies among adopted adults that showed a clear pattern of under-achievement.

A lawyer in California was advocating open adoption, with the natural mother meeting the adoptive parents *before* the child was born. The natural mother would then have the security of knowing the environment in which her child was being placed, and the adoptive parents would be in a far better position to answer the inevitable questions asked by their adopted child about his natural parents. This was in direct opposition to the secrecy advocated by adoption agencies who give both sets of parents only token information.

Where else in our free society was such secrecy condoned?

I knew that the question of a natural mother's right to privacy (which enables her to make a new life) is one of the three principles upon which the sealed records are defended—the other two being the child's right to a secure childhood and the right of the adoptive parents to build a home free from the fear that the natural mother will return to claim her child.

I could understand that the latter two principles genuinely *protect*—at a vulnerable period and at no one's expense.

I could also understand the possible plight of the natural mother, who had once given up her child and might, many years later, suddenly become vulnerable to exposure and even harassment and blackmail. But privacy from whom? *Her own child?*

And what about that child, the innocent silent party in a legal action that decided *forever* what he would be entitled to know about his heredity? Why *forever*? Did the mother's right to secrecy include the right to condemn *her* child to a lifetime of silence?

It was a hard question.

There seemed so much work to be done before the dilemma would be fully understood. I began to wonder whether the experience I'd gained during my years of searching might not be put to some constructive use.

I heard a radio rebuttal by an attorney, Lorraine Israel, to one station's editorial defending the "adoptive parents" of "Baby Lenore" and the proposed thirty-day surrender bill. So impressed was I by the perception, sensitivity, and *sanity* of her statement that I phoned the station for her address. I called her immediately and thanked her for having had the courage to speak out.

"I just feel that it's criminal what they're doing. Thirty days is ludicrous!" She then told me that she was sponsoring another bill, which she had helped write. It asked that the court appoint a "law guardian" where a natural mother could not afford counsel to represent and advise her of all her rights before she gave up her child—and that natural mothers have six to nine months in which to rescind their surrenders before adoptions become final. Under the New York State law of 1971 under which the Baby Lenore case was being tried, she said an adoption could not become final before six months after a surrender, but that once a mother had surrendered her child she would have to show she was fit and competent before she could get her child back.

I learned so much during that conversation. Curious, I asked Lorraine if she had been adopted.

"No," she said.

"I was adopted," I said, "and when I heard your statement it was as though you had known what I was thinking and feeling all my life."

"Why don't you come down for lunch tomorrow and let's talk about it," Lorraine said.

My mother had not contacted me after our evening together at the Beekman Tower. Periodically, as summer passed into fall, I would think of her. Her birthday came and went; I was tempted to make her something pretty but decided against it. No relationship that is forced can ever be meaningful, and I felt my mother must take the initiative.

October passed into November. Several weeks later, in early December, the phone rang.

I knew at once who it was. "How are you?"

"You've been sending me messages," she said, "I couldn't sleep last night."

From then on, my mother began to phone regularly. Sometimes she'd go home from the office during her lunch hour and we'd talk for twenty minutes, or she'd rush home after work and we'd talk for an hour. We chatted on a wide variety of subjects, neither dwelling on nor avoiding the topic of adoption, and were becoming friends.

She told me she was so proud of what I had done with my life, and it saddened her to think she'd had no part in it. "I get up every morning, look in the mirror and see your face," she said. "I want to tell the world, 'this is my daughter,' and I'm ashamed of myself; I don't have the courage." She still had not told the family.

We met for lunch at a Chinese restaurant near her office, ordered shrimp with lobster sauce simultaneously, and laughed. I was wearing a turquoise dress I designed myself. She admired it and remarked that turquoise was one of her favorite colors—turquoise and lavender. They were also mine. She had brought old family pictures to show me, told me of my great-grandparents in Russia, how my grandmother had smoked gold-tipped cigarettes—bits and pieces of information that delighted me. I told her

of my travels abroad, my love for Italy, and said lightly
that my one disappointment in finding my real family was
that they were Russian, not Italian!

Later she said, "It's ironic that the one person with
whom I can share my innermost feelings is the child I
gave away." She paused for a moment and took out a
cigarette. "Florence, I know now that I will never be able
to tell the family," she said, tension coming into her voice.
"They'll turn from me."

It wasn't telling her husband she feared. She was sure
he would love me simply because I was a part of her. It
was my brother and sister—she just could not bring herself
to gamble on their reaction. They had never been told of
her early marriage.

As we left the restaurant I put my hand on the door
to open it for her. Her voice breaking, she said: "Can I
just hold you . . . for a minute?" I came closer to her
and she put her arms around me and held me very tight.

By the time I arrived home that evening, a light snow
had begun to fall. The phone was ringing as I opened
the door. It was my mother, asking me if I had gotten
home all right.

"I'm all right," I said gently.

"Did you get your feet wet?"

"No," I said with a laugh.

"I just want you to know," she said, "that I think you're
beautiful, and that I love you very much."

Early one afternoon shortly after my lunch with my
mother, Lorraine called. The thirty-day bill was coming
up soon and passage seemed assured. "I can't stand this
any longer," she said. "I've got to do something. I'm going
to Albany to speak with the legislators. It probably won't
do any good, but anything is better than sitting passively
and watching them ramrod this thirty-day horror through.
Want to keep me company?"

"When are you going?" I asked.

"Tonight."

"I'll go," I said.

Lorraine had nothing to gain from such a trip. She had seen what she thought was a terrible wrong and had to do something, however small, to correct it.

Were Lorraine and I the only ones in the entire state to feel the injustice of what was happening? We were like helpless bystanders in that horrible scene from *Zorba the Greek,* where a woman is stoned by the town. Our chances of stopping the bill, we knew, were nil—but still we had to try.

As the bus headed out of the city toward Albany that icy March evening, we looked at each other and laughed. I said: "We're crazy. Absolutely crazy."

I had always viewed myself as apolitical. It was inconceivable that I was actually on my way to Albany to argue with trained politicians, most of whom had already made up their minds.

We found several legislators in their rooms that evening and talked to them until three or four in the morning, pleading with them to wait until the furor over the Baby Lenore case died down before considering such a change in the law.

We didn't get to sleep until six A.M., and when Lorraine woke me an hour later I could barely stand I was so tired. I had four cups of black coffee, found a free typewriter in the capitol building, and wrote a letter to the legislators asking them not to pass a bill that would sever a child from its mother within thirty days. I said that by giving the mother a chance they were giving the child a chance, not merely to have *a* home, but *the* home that gave him hereditary continuity. You cannot legislate against nature, I said. The one thing we cannot share with our adoptive parents, nor they with us, is our ancestry. If there is no alternative, then give adoption every chance to work, but first try to keep the child with its natural mother.

I never realized I'd had the thoughts that tumbled out of my brain so easily.

When I finished typing the letter, Lorraine and I had it mimeographed, and then distributed copies in the mail room to each member of the legislature. After this we went back to the legislators, going from office to office, trying with quiet reason to change their minds. Most of them admitted they knew none of the actual details of the Baby Lenore case, nor of the procedure of adoption; "heredity" and "identity" were new words to them in this context. Some admitted they could see the points we were making and honestly had never considered them. Others said our position had much validity, but their votes for passage of the bill were "committed."

Lorraine spotted one of the backers of the bill and asked if we could sit down and talk it over for a few minutes. Better still, why not have a public hearing on it?

"It's as good as passed," he said, refusing any further discussion or consideration of a public hearing.

We came to a room in which several legislators had gathered. I forced myself to walk up to them and said: "Please . . . think of what you're doing." I told them I was an adopted child who had spent half her life looking for her parents and her identity; I told them that the practice of adoption as it exists in America today consigns the child to lifelong anonymity. "Before you pass this law, why not gather together a group of adoptees and ask us how we feel? Who, after all, is more important in adoption than the child? Whose interests should be paramount?" I suggested that adopted children were told they were chosen, but wasn't adoption really a *second choice* for the adoptive parents, resorted to only when they could not have their biological children? "Please, give the child an opportunity to remain with its natural parent. The adopted infant is no blank slate . . . he brings his chromosomes with him. Don't deny his heredity."

Suddenly a politician thrust his face near mine and

screamed at me. "Heredity, bullshit!" The spray from his words slapped against my cheek. I jumped back. "You're psychotic. You're an isolated case. Not one in a thousand goes looking!"

After he was gone, one of the legislators who had witnessed the scene told us that the man was an *adoptive father*.

All the way home on the bus I couldn't forget those words. I told Lorraine he might just as well have been saying, "Heredity, bullshit" to his own child.

We were both exhausted. Lorraine, who had been through days like this before, could ride with the blows; she turned off and went to sleep.

I curled up in a back seat and tried to sleep, but could not. My eyes were riveted open. I could think of nothing but that man's words.

I had frozen, too shocked to reply to him. *You are the last person who is ever going to talk to me like that again,* I thought. *I'm going to find out if other adopted people feel as I do. If his is the prevailing attitude, we need all the help we can get!*

─●─

dult who was an adopted child desires contact with
her adoptees to exchange views on adoptive situation
d for mutual assistance in search for natural parents.

he morning after my ad appeared in *The New York
imes,* my mother called and said: "I saw your ad in the
per yesterday. You placed that ad, didn't you?"

I said: "Yes, I did."

"I knew as soon as I read it that it was you," she said.
could tell it had disturbed her. "Florence, you're opening
Pandora's box."

"It's got to be opened," I said. "It's time we faced the
oblems." I could feel a terrible decision pressing on me.
y mother still could not bear the thought of any pub-
ity; she wanted the best of both worlds: a back-door
lationship with me and privacy from the rest of the
orld. I felt when I placed the ad I might be setting
mething in motion I would be unable to stop. I did not
ow what the response would be, but sensed I was be-
ming involved in something much larger than myself.

I wanted to have a relationship with my mother, but open and free, not covert and surreptitious. I had not yet called her "mother." In fact, for all our recent intimacy, I had never called her *anything*. I would *not* call her by her first name. She would have to choose whether to hide and retreat as she had done for more than forty years. I was afraid I'd have to choose between what was becoming in my mind "the adoption cause" and my own mother.

I placed ads in several New York newspapers and I was soon inundated by mail from all parts of the country. I was totally unprepared to answer the literally thousands of letters that poured in.

Several of the first letters were from adoptive parents. Some of these were threatening; one said simply, "Don't place that ad again!" and another: "You should have been an abortion not an adoption." But the same day, this letter arrived: "Son—(perhaps if you were mine I'd call you 'Son' but I'll call you that because you're not mine but all of ours). . . .

"I have thought of nothing else since reading your ad. You see, almost eight years ago I gave birth to a little baby boy—out of wedlock. He was given up for adoption —and my heart has never healed. I wanted that baby more than life itself. I could have aborted him but I wanted that life inside me to live.

"I was twenty-three then. I was raised by a very devout Catholic family. I fell in love with a divorced man and together my son was conceived. He wanted very much to marry me—but my parents wouldn't have it. They sent me away to an unwed mothers' home—and there I lived alone, ashamed and an outcast from the Church and what we call 'society.'

"When my time came, labor was hard and swift and my son was about his business in getting born in time for spring. I remember the smile—almost a frozen grin when the doctor said, 'It's a boy!' I insisted upon seeing him—for I wanted him with me as long as possible. Most of the girls felt it would be easier not to see the sons and daughters that shared life with them in this particular suspension of time. But I wanted mine—he was mine, he is mine, and every moment was worth more and was more precious than a house of ten children born in wedlock. I remember going to the nursery window every day and watching you with your kimono pinned up because you had scratched your right cheek, which held two dimples (the only identification mark I know, should we ever meet again). I remember staring through that glass alone, surrounded by fathers and uncles and aunts and friends, admiring all those babies around you. And I looked at you, with no father, no aunts, no uncles, no friends to say how beautiful you were, and then I carefully looked over at all those safe, secure little blankets of pink and blue and I wanted you to have their kinds of chances. Why shouldn't you, poor little guy—you have been through more in your unborn time than perhaps they would go through all their lives. But somehow I just knew that you would be better because of it. And so, my tiny little blue blanket, we left that hospital together for the first and last time. In that big black limousine from the adoption agency we drove on into the city, over the bridge, me in the back seat with you in my arms, we drove into 'Society's World' where you would be accepted and become the fine boy I'm sure you are.

"You were christened 'Danny Boy,' after the Irish song, and perhaps one day you will come and find me in the place where I am lying and say an 'Ave' over me.

Love,
Mother"

The week the first letters arrived I called a number of people from the New York area who had responded to my ad. All were looking for their parents, and most of them were terribly concerned about two things: that, as I had felt with Uncle Abe, they would hurt their adoptive parents and that their natural mothers would not want to see them. I read the letter to them, and they were as moved as I had been. Together we placed a second ad in *The New York Times*. It read:

> To Danny Boy's Mother—
> You're not just his, but all of ours.

Shortly after it appeared, she wrote to me again: "To My Sons—To My Daughters,

"As I take my pen in hand, I pause to think how very sweet that you would want to hear from me again. It brings a pang to my heart, a tear to my eyes, and a smile to my lips.

"I remember once last summer when I was visiting friends in Vermont, we were in the town square reading the local bulletin board when I felt a tugging at my dress. There stood a small boy just about the age my son would be. He began to talk to me—and I kept staring at him while he proceeded to tell me all about the pickle the man in the grocery store gave him for being such a good boy. I kept trying to remember in those few moments my baby's face—with the two dimples on his cheek. I became so fascinated by him—I thought it was a miracle that of all those people reading the bulletin board—about fifteen or so—he should want to speak to me.

"I thought, 'Oh, God—he's my son! Thank God, at last I have found him.' But soon his aunt came and as he took her hand I wanted to cry out—to take him in my arms and never let them separate us again. I followed them for as long as I could and soon they got into a station wagon and drove away. If I had not been on foot I would have followed.

"A mother never forgets—no mother, whoever she is— no matter how many other babies she may bear. There is always the longing, the wondering—the hope—that one day you may be together again.

"That's why I think it's so wonderful, so humane, and so very necessary to understand each of us. My only hope is that one day my 'Danny Boy' will find me—and 'you' are my hope—my light in the darkness. I know the words from my lips are conveying the wish of your own mother and the thousands of others like us.

"Someday, and you never give up hope, the knock will come on the door—and in one solitary moment all the years of separation, tears, prayers, and searching will be over. Perhaps it will all be because of you.

"I kiss you gently, hug you tightly, and wish you and our cause much success. Whenever you listen to the words to 'Danny Boy,' you will know that each of us is waiting for each of you.

> All my love,
> *Mother*"

The following week I arranged a meeting of all the people I could contact in the New York area. If I could develop an organization, we'd need a name, and I wanted one with true meaning. After several days of serious thought, I worked out Adoptees' Liberty Movement Association, or ALMA; *alma* is the Spanish word for "soul." Our slogan would be: "The truth of his origin is the birthright of every man." We would accept no minors, and our concern would be to make the records available to adult adoptees. We would encourage research so that those adoptees who come after us, and their parents—both natural and adoptive—will benefit from the legacy of our experiences.

Only five people came to our first meeting, held on a Sunday in early April; but a week later, eleven people showed up. Thereafter, as word got around, our meetings had a larger and larger attendance, not to mention the thousands of people from states as far-flung as California and Alaska who sent in a small dues payment, their good wishes, and their pleas for help. I decided early that it would be wrong to search for other adoptees' parents for them. If someone really wants to look—and not everybody does—it's healthier for them to do so themselves. I have now seen many who sought and found and grew confident in the process.

We at ALMA do not persuade our members to search. When they come to us they have already made their decisions. Recently we have begun to keep a complete card file of all who are looking—adoptees, natural parents, sisters and brothers who have been separated by adoption, and adoptive parents who are interested in helping their children locate their natural parents. The file is arranged chronologically by birth dates, to enable us to match parents and children.

One New York newspaper, which had enthusiastically defended the prospective adoptive parents in the Baby Lenore case refused to accept my ad on the grounds that "We can't control what happens as a result of an ad like this." Finally I called a columnist at this paper. He was unprepared for my onslaught. "Your paper's 'Inquiring Reporter' asks garbage collectors, the man on the street, everyone and anyone about the Baby Lenore case. Why not ask those most concerned?"

"How can we ask the babies?"

"Some of these 'babies,' as you put it, are now parents and even grandparents," I said. "You can ask us." I told him I had found my mother after a search that had lasted half my life—did that qualify me to answer questions?

"Have you given your story to anyone else?" he asked.

"No," I said.

"Will you give it to me?"

After he heard my story he suggested I take a box number. I told him I couldn't see why.

"Well," he said, "you might get some adverse mail."

His article was quite sympathetic to my position. The next day, and for days afterward, I was deluged with hundreds and hundreds of letters from that paper's vast readership. As the columnist had predicted some of it was "adverse."

"They should have left you in the gutter," one letter said.

One woman, who signed her letter, "A Loving Adopted Mother," wrote: "We have enough trouble in this world without you stirring up any more. You make me sick."

Still another said: "It's a shame that some potential parent might be denied the experience of parenthood by listening to the sick ideas of a woman like you. And it's a cruel act on your part to make it sound as if all adopted children are as neurotic, maladjusted, and as searching as you are."

There were more letters like this, and it made me sad to think that the adverse mail came *only* from adoptive parents, adults who presumably had adopted babies for the good of the children, who held their children's welfare foremost. "After reading the article," another said, "I have become more convinced that abortion is the best answer for an unwanted pregnancy. As repugnant as it is to me to take away a little life that has hardly begun, it is more repugnant to me to have that life grow up and after being loved and adopted never being able to accept this love as it is. The person who has given birth is *not* the mother— the adoptive parents who have loved, nursed, worked, sacrificed, worried, and cared for the child all the growing years are the Mother and Father!"

"My baby is *my* baby," another adoptive parent said. "Her natural or birth mother is *nonexistent* . . . I can understand about heritage. But let me tell you this: it's just *you*—because naturally I do not feel anything about my 'heritage,' good or bad." And another: "Adoptive parents give *more* love to their children than regular parents do. You are nothing but ungrateful."

One adoptive parent spoke plainly of the fear she felt: "Of course it's frightening to think that perhaps one day an adopted child will search for her or his natural parents."

Why, I wondered, should this be so frightening? Where a loving and textured relationship exists, how could it not continue—and remain as strong whether an adoptee looked or didn't look? Why couldn't they trust their love —and that of their adopted children for them?

Some of these adoptive parents denied heredity yet seemed positively to hate the natural mother of their children and to assume that the child, conceived in sin and ugliness, owed all that was bad in it to its origins, and had only one respectable course for the rest of his life, unstinting gratitude to his adoptive parents. "You were lousy from the day you were brought into this world, and you are lousier now that you are a grown woman. If your real mother really wanted you she would have found a way to keep you, but she did not want to keep you. If your real mother was any good she would not have gotten into trouble. She knew what she was doing when she got into trouble. You should get on your hands and knees and thank God up above for your wonderful adoptive parents."

"You are thinking *only* of the *adopted child,*" said an adoptive mother. "You seem to have completely forgotten the adoptive parents. Where do they fit in your wild scheme?"

I also received some very different letters from adoptive parents, men and women who wanted to understand more about the tenuous triangle—natural parents, adoptive parents, adoptees. They recognized that my object was *more* love and understanding, not less—and that my experience might lead them to a true knowledge of their own roles and the needs of their children. "I am a psychologist interested primarily in child development and child behavior disorders," one man wrote. "Also, I happen to be an adoptive parent. . . . As such I have read with great interest your statements. I happen to agree wholeheartedly with your organization's ideas. My conviction is, as a father, and from what I know as a child psychologist, that it is very important for adopted children to be able to gain a feeling of their biological identities."

"Why should I deny my daughter the right to share her adult life with her blood relations?" an adoptive mother asked. "This might bring much happiness to all involved, including me. What would make her happy would add to my happiness." Yes. And her child would love her even *more* for her warmth and understanding.

Some parents, though they were concerned about the "other parents," kept the needs of their children paramount. "As the mother of an adopted daughter, I have worried ever since we became her parents about the time when she would need to know about her roots and family background. . . . If those natural parents were willing, I would love my daughter to know them, too, whenever in her life she might want to."

As the year wore on, I was called upon to participate in a variety of television and radio panels, conferences of social workers, and newspaper interviews; I received invitations from various state adoption services centers, departments of public welfare, and a religious child and family service that "believes strongly that a child who has been adopted has a right to his history." In one eastern state, social workers were so convinced by the presentation I made that they agreed to give adults over eighteen who were adopted through their agency access to their records simply upon request. Scotland allows adoptees the right of access to all records and information concerning their adoptions at age seventeen. In all but a very few states in the United States the adopted adult, of any age, is denied the right to see the true records of his birth and adoption.

ALMA has as one of its principal goals the opening of records to any adopted person *over eighteen* who wants, for any reason, to see them. An adult has the *right* to know. Several interviews that led to major articles in *The New York Times, Coronet* magazine, and elsewhere brought a further barrage of letters from across the country. It was gratifying to find that most of them felt they had found a friend, an ally, a confidante—someone who had lived what they had lived. I was, frankly, astounded that there were so many adoptees who felt as I felt.

One letter I might have written myself had I still been searching:

"I have spent some twenty-odd years in a desperate drive to find and know my ancestry. Pouring my heart and soul out to my family—begging and pleading for facts about my natural parents. I had literally drained myself of all emotion trying to make them understand my need to know. I received neither their support nor their understanding. I grew up in a state of mourning over the loss of myself—over the loss of my identity.

"I married—gave birth—miracles to me. Yet even the happiness of a marriage filled with love and fulfilled by children couldn't mask the unhappiness I suffered by not knowing my true identity. Today, whether it be by chance or by the help of God, I saw your discussion on television about people wanting to know who their natural parents are. This is unbelievable to me. I have spent twenty years of my life trying to get someone to understand and suddenly today you understand."

Others also stressed how important it was for them to find someone who understood; few of them had had the concrete success I had. But I could see deeper, with each letter, into the springs of my search. "You were like an answer to a prayer." "Today's article, revealing the existence of ALMA, was both a surprise and a delight." "It was an absolutely thrilling experience to find someone saying the things that I have been thinking for such a long time." "It is heartbreaking that we are denied the most important things in our lives, our right to know who we are. Thirty-six years of searching and finally all I came up with is a copy of the adoption—just two last names, which I've known for quite some time." "I always thought I was alone in my curiosity about my natural mother and father. . . . How fantastic it would be to find out something about my background and heredity. Also, perhaps my own mother is curious about me and has tried to find me, but also thought it was impossible."

Perhaps the most telling phrase of them all was the simple: "It is always there, in the back of my mind. *Please help me if you can!*"

I was particularly interested in learning that so many adopted people who deeply loved their adoptive parents still wanted to meet their natural mothers. This letter is typical: "The most wonderful thing of all is that I was really loved—and I knew it. On top of all that, my parents loved each other very much. . . . Now with all that love in my family, one might ask, 'Why would she even care about her natural mother?' My answer to that question is this—I want to see if I resemble her in any way and I'm terribly curious to know the whys and wherefores concerning my being put up for adoption. I would *never* disrupt her life."

Simple curiosity? Yes, it is that. And it is normal. But it is also a "tremendous" undefinable need to discover one's own heritage . . . good or bad, but one's *own*.

One of the most interesting facets of ALMA meetings is the way natural mothers and adoptees gravitate toward each other. The natural parents, worried that their children might reject or resent them, see that they have never been resented; the adoptees, when they talk to the natural mothers, lose some of their deep fears that they will be rejected when they find their real mothers.

Many adoptees have been told by social workers and adoption agencies and their adoptive parents that the search is evidence of mental instability. Certainly many adoptees have problems. Dr. Zellig Bach, a leading clinical psychologist who has worked extensively with adoptive children, speaks of the learning blocks adoptees often have—and I had one myself; he stresses that since the most basic facts of their lives—knowledge of their parents

—was denied them, or distorted, other facts don't matter.

Studies by Dr. Alexina Mary McWhinnie show conclusively that adoptees who reported little adjustment problems were the ones who had freedom of discussion and exploration at home—and parents who had answers and were willing to share them. The search for natural parents is a simple and elemental need, which is called "adolescent" and worse—but usually by those who *know* their natural parents. *Not knowing* makes all the difference.

One adoptee, speaking of the virtual conspiracy she felt on the part of her adoptive parents and the agencies and social workers, said: "They tell parents what to tell us, how to tell us, when to tell us, and of course how much to tell us. One can only conclude that we are some special breed of people not entitled to be aware of our own history and origins."

Soon after ALMA got under way, my mother called me and said: "I want to see you, even if it's only one more time." I knew then—and I believe she knew—that decisions were pressing upon us both.

We did not meet again. We have never met since that day we had lunch together in the Chinese restaurant.

We spoke by phone a number of times and then, when I was scheduled to appear on a national television talk show, she saw the listing and called to ask me not to use my real name on the show. No decision was harder for me to make. I told her that to do this would negate everything I had worked for, everything I stood for. "I've dropped my adoptive name," I said. "It's not me. I can't use my married name because of the hate mail."

I wanted to protect my mother. But I had fought for my real name and my heritage and I would not deny them, not even for her.

She was upset so I called her back soon afterward.

"Please forgive me," she said. "Don't hate me."

"How could I hate you?" I asked. "And what is there to forgive?"

"I can't"—her voice began to crack—"I can't bear the thought . . . of anyone knowing."

I knew now that the choice really was not mine but my mother's. I knew I couldn't give up ALMA. The letters pleading for understanding came in every day, from all over the country. These were people who had been lied to and kept in darkness, who felt strengthened after all these years by an organization dedicated to helping them. I would not abandon them.

"Mother, tell the family the truth," I told her as gently as I could. "Not for me but for you. Because you have said that my grandmother is reaching out through the grave to hurt you. As long as you live a lie then she still has power over you. The moment you tell the truth she can't touch you anymore."

She was silent.

"Mother?" I said.

"Forgive me," she said. "I don't want to interfere in your life."

"I know. You're not rejecting me. You're rejecting . . . life and truth. Please understand. I must use my real name. That's who I am. I will no longer be what others have told me to be," I said. "I love you."

And then we said good-bye.

Eighteen

Anyone knowing the whereabouts of Frederick I.
Fisher, son of Jacob Fisher and Irene Cornfeld Fisher,
please contact Florence . . . .

It was May and spring created an atmosphere filled with
promise. I knew the time had come to resume the search
for my father.

My mother had told me that a year after my birth she
had accidentally run into my paternal grandfather in New
York. She said he had seemed genuinely concerned about
me and my welfare, so I decided to start with him. I went
through the city directories but found no trace of him.

Shortly after my first radio interview, a Philadelphia
doctor and his wife who had heard the program and who
were sympathetic sent the first small contribution to
ALMA. When I wrote them that I was coming to Philadelphia to search for my father they reserved a room for
me at the Bellevue-Stratford Hotel, filled it with candy
and fruit, and arranged for the bill to be sent to them.
Although we had never met before, we became friends over

dinner that evening. They created a mood of optimism that remained with me the next few days.

The next morning I set out to see the city records. I checked through forty years of births, deaths, wills, letters of probate, divorces, annulments, voting registration, drivers licenses, criminal records. I even checked marriage licenses from the time of my parents' separation through 1970. My theory was that if my dad was the man my mother had said he was, his chances of remarrying were pretty good!

I found only my mother and father's original wedding license. And, of course, unable to resist ringing doorbells, I went to Chestnut Street.

Nothing.

But I did find *something*. For the first time in all those years of searching. *Kindness. Everywhere.* A kindness and a willingness to help on the part of everyone I encountered.

Nobody vanishes. A red-headed man should be easy to find. Everybody leaves a trace. Everybody it seemed, but Frederick I. Fisher with *his* red hair and laughing blue-gray eyes.

My mother had told me she thought my father's family came from a Jersey town beginning with a "V," probably Vineland, and that there were four or five brothers. I phoned a funeral director in Vineland named Victor Rone, and asked if he would check his burial records and direct me to the neighboring Jewish cemeteries. I told him I was coming to Vineland on Saturday. He asked if I would like him to contact some Fishers and place an ad in the community paper. Although he sounded sincere, when I hung up I almost forgot our conversation: I'd heard dozens of empty promises.

It was now Thursday, May 6. I returned to New York neither discouraged nor disheartened, merely determined.

Stan and I were having dinner that evening, discussing my next strategy, when the phone rang. Stan answered.

He said, "Yes, she's here, just a moment . . ." and his face went pale.

I knew. Silently I mouthed the words as he handed me the receiver, *"It's about my father."*

"My name is Ben Fisher," the voice said. "I'm your uncle. Your father is living in California . . . and . . ."

Over, over, it's all over . . . I dropped the phone and ran from the room sobbing.

I could hear Stan carrying on a quiet conversation with my uncle. I composed myself, went back into the kitchen, and took the receiver again. I listened unbelieving as Uncle Ben told me that Victor Rone himself had begun to call all the twenty-one Fishers in Vineland for me. He had also placed the ad in the community paper. One of my many cousins had seen it and in no time the entire town knew someone was looking for Uncle Fred—his *daughter.*

"I don't know what my brother thinks or feels," my uncle said. "He's been an actor and stunt man in Hollywood since you were born. We rarely see each other. But you have a right to find him. So take his number and call him now."

I said, "You mean *just call him?*"

"Sure, just call him. He's a big boy. He can take it. So, don't waste time talking to me, call your father, and Florence, you have a family now—after you've spoken to your dad I'll tell you all about them."

I went into the bedroom, sat down on the bed near the telephone, and for a long time just stared at the number I had written down. Then I dialed the operator, repeated the number twice to make sure she got it right, asked to speak person-to-person with *Frederick Fisher,* and waited.

Please let him be there.

The operator asked for Frederick Fisher, and I heard my father's voice. It was just as my mother had remem-

Epilogue

A young man recently stood outside a funeral home for two full days, searching the face of each person who went in or out. He had seen a death notice in the newspaper, and he was hoping he'd see someone who looked like him. He wanted desperately to find one of his relatives, the first blood relative he'd ever have seen. He was hoping the dead man was his grandfather.

This young man will, now and then, call me late in the evening to tell me the progress of his search. Periodically he now rents a car—which he can ill afford—and drives more than an hour to the home of a woman he is *almost* sure is his mother. He doesn't know with nearly the certainty that I knew.

I have seen this man's records, and the possibility exists; it is a distinct possibility, no more. He asks me whether the time has come to confront this woman, to speak to her; he suggests ringing her bell and passing himself off as an insurance investigator. I tell him to wait. I tell him to get more proof. He sits in the parked car, across the street from the comfortable suburban home, for hours—hoping for a glimpse of the woman he thinks is his mother. He does not want to disturb her, just to see her.

I spoke to an adoptive parents' group not long ago. The seats were filled to capacity and the standing room around the seats was full, too. At one point I suggested that records be opened at age eighteen. Instantly there was bedlam. When the room grew quiet, I asked them simply: "Do you want *your* child to go through the hell I went through?" I was not reaching into their homes to steal their children; I am a mother myself. But I think of the letters I receive daily, and of my own search, and of that young man sitting outside a home in which he thinks, maybe, perhaps, his natural mother lives.

How much there still is to learn about the whole phenomenon of adoption!

Even today, when most enlightened adoptive parents tell their children about the *fact* of their adoption, many feel resentment—and personal failure—if that child asks questions or actually goes out on The Search. "The fact is that an adoptive child has two pairs of parents," says Dr. R. G. Deibel, Director of the Federation for Unmarried Mothers in Holland: "those who were unable to take care of it, and those who do have this privilege. Give the child this positive view of its status and you will give it a basis for integrating the existence of two pairs of parents into its life in a well-balanced manner. Then it will be able to find its identity." How much sadness would be avoided if Dr. Deibel's view were really understood and fully accepted.

I am not by nature an activist. I love music and literature; I prefer to make a handbag than to make a speech. Friends sometimes ask me why I continue my involvement with the problem of adoption after having found both my parents. I cannot do otherwise. Not while there are sealed records and sealed minds. Everyone is somebody's child. Everyone has a history—and that history can neither be denied nor ignored. All acts have consequences. There is a third party to every adoption, and that child has every right to pursue the truth about his own life. He did not simply grow; he grew in someone's womb and has a hereditary history. It is as useless to deny this as it once was to say the world is flat.

Each day I receive dozens more letters. Another article appears, and is perhaps syndicated, and my desk is again flooded. A certain portion of it is adverse mail; but the overwhelming proportion is from adoptees—who simply *want to know*.

One tells me her child is dying, and the doctors think it may be a hereditary disease. While they worked around the clock, she went to the adoption agency—and learned no more than that she had "two parents." Agencies are not required by law to maintain such confidentiality, yet they do so as a matter of policy. If, as they profess, the *child* is their true client, why when that child becomes adult do they undermine his right to the truth about his life?

Another—a seventeen-year-old, unwed and well-pregnant—wanted to save her child. The agencies had persuaded her, and her parents had persuaded her, that the child's welfare would best be met by giving her child up for adoption. Abortion or adoption. These are the only choices they gave her. I made some calls; some members of ALMA warmly encouraged her to keep her child when it was born, and even offered to take her child for a year, while she got on her feet. She finally decided to keep her baby, and a year later she married—and all was well.

One woman writes: "I am now seventy-eight years old and my only wish is to have some contact with the child I gave up for adoption before I pass on. Can you help me?"

The letters come by the hundreds. Some days I can't open them. *Enough. I can't bear to read them anymore.* I let them sit on my desk, sixty or seventy of them, unopened. They stay there for two days and then three. I look at the piles of unopened letters, piles that grow larger every day, from every section of the country.

And then I think of all the years I was alone. I think of how I had to beg and search. I remember how I sought only one other person who would understand.

We pass this way but once. We make a mockery of life if we do not pursue our dreams, if we hedge against reality and know but half of what we are.

I take a small batch of letters and begin to open them, one by one, each a bit of another human being's soul. The first and last of them say, simply: "All I want to know is what everyone else knows—and takes for granted: my roots."

ALMA (Adoptees' Liberty Movement Association)
P. O. Box 154
Washington Bridge Station
New York, New York 10033